THE CALL FOR
REVIVALISTS

David Edwards

FOREWORD BY ALLESSIA EDWARDS

D1359809

ENDORSEMENTS

"But you shall receive power when the Holy Spirit has come upon you; and you shall be witnesses to Me in Jerusalem, and in all Judea and Samaria and to the ends of the earth," Acts 1:8.

On June 6, 1995, I received a baptism of power and fire that transformed my life and began the journey of what is now a Kingdom Family Movement that is spreading the flames of revival all over the world. Through this movement, David Edwards became a spiritual son and is a revivalist that God has raised up for such a time as this.

David is full of passion, power, and purity. The Call for Revivalists is available for anyone who desires to be part of the greatest revival the world has ever seen. There is no longer an excuse to limit God and how he wants to use you. I encourage you to be one of the burning ones that will burn brightly without burning out. Receiving, becoming and spreading revival fire is the upgrade we all desire—say yes to the call!

LEIF HETLAND
President & Founder, Global Mission Awareness
Author, *Called to Reign, Giant Slayers, Seeing Through Heaven's Eyes*

I'm so impressed and inspired by David Edwards. He is the message written on the pages of this book. With eager and happy anticipation of eternal impact, I recommend his brilliant work.

JENN STOCKMAN
First Year Director, Bethel Atlanta School of Supernatural Ministry

David Edwards is a friend and former student who faithfully carries the fire of God as a torch for his generation. I deeply appreciate and respect his burden for the church to be revived to her fullness. We need more people like him. His desire to see the Kingdom come begins in his home and extends to the nations. I highly commend him and his message.

ROBERT GLADSTONE, PhD

Senior Leader, The King's People
Professor of Practical Theology, FIRE School of Ministry

David Edwards is a very passionate prophetic leader. He is focused and committed to continuing the growth of the prophetic gift on his life. He has an extensive knowledge of the Word of God that shows in his application of Scripture in this book. His ability to train and equip the body through writing from a foundation of a victorious eschatology is both refreshing and empowering. Dave's heart to help people hear the voice of God and respond to what he is saying is very needed in the church.

This book will both equip you to walk in and understand the commission to expand the Kingdom in this day and age. Dave is not just a fellow leader; he is also a great friend of mine and my physical trainer. I can honestly say that Dave does not just preach an empty message, but fully lives by the revelation God has released over his life and has the testimony that follows in his work, ministry, and personal life. I wholeheartedly endorse David Edwards and his ministry.

SCOTT THOMPSON

Lead Pastor, Lifehouse Eureka
Author, *Words of Knowledge Made Easy*

David Edwards has done a great job in capturing the heart of God regarding the subjects of Revival and Revivalists. In this new book, he does more than just bring these subjects to the surface for review and nostalgic conversation; he, in fact, presents these all-important subjects in such a way that it brings every reader to a decision as to how they will live their lives going forward in Christ! I fully recommend and encourage all to read this book!"

KEITH COLLINS

Founder, Generation Impact Ministries
Director, FIRE School of Ministry

In *The Call for Revivalists*, David Edwards trumpets again an ancient call that has been heard by burning hearts throughout history. It's the call that ignited the hearts of two disciples the road to Emmaus. It is the call that drove John the Baptist into the wilderness, and the call that beckoned him out of that solitary place to "prepare ye the way of The Lord!" This manuscript describes not only the wonder of this call, but also offers a practical bridge from living in the mundane to daily experiencing the miraculous. Dave's personal stories of his journey demonstrate that we ALL can go there! We all have the same privilege to cohabit Heaven and Earth; it's just a matter of priorities. Many receive this call, but only a few will answer. As men jockey for position in the Kingdom, God seems to notice the first one to his knees...Dave's knees are calloused, and you can tell!

JON POTTER

Lead Pastor, Canvas Church
Author, *Spiritual Identity Fraud: Restoring God's Sons and Daughters*

David Edwards is a rising voice to a new generation of revivalists. His passion for authentic revival is contagious. As you read this book, you will be challenged and ignited to seek after the heart of God even more. I highly recommend this book to all who are hungry for more of God.

SCOTT NARY
Founder, 420 Fire Ministries
Author, *Power Evangelism: Activating a Jesus Lifestyle*

There's a generation of firebrands rising up, stepping into their identity as sons and daughters. David Edwards is at the forefront, leading the charge. The heart of the Kingdom of God is revival, and the instruments God uses are revivalists. Dave lives to see the "restoration of all things." He models a life whereby those who are surrendered are weapons of love brandished to defeat principalities and powers. This book encourages a lifestyle of fire that spreads into every sphere. I recommend this book to those both daring and desiring to be used by God to touch and transform the world. Let Dave help you unlock the divine realities of Heaven as a lifestyle in these pages.

PETER PUTNAM
Evangelist, Speaker, Champion Bodybuilder

CONTENTS

ALLESSIA

You are my love, my wife, my whole world.

We were created to share the journey together. I cherish every sweet moment I have with you. You are the reason this book has become a reality. I forever love you, my dear.

I delight in you!

RECOGNITION

Heavenly Family is a key message in my life and a key theme in this book. We are His body, His dear ones, His Family. Everyone in His Family is in my Family. And, as the Family of God in the Earth, Heaven is not just a destination, but it is who we are.

This book represents 20 years of following Jesus, with all the trials and triumphs along the way. Many have stood by me, loved me, encouraged me, helped me to be patient, and pushed me forward. Each season of life adds new friends, mentors, heroes, and those who become lifers. Each one is God-given and holds a special place in my heart.

To my Dad, Tabby, and Adam, I smile when I think of you. Thanks for encouraging me in both editions of this book and persuading me to keep the title the same. It makes the book right. Damian McCrink, you're persistent and loving friendship allowed me to open my heart and let Jesus in. Brandon, without your love for God, I would've been in thirst. You showed me how to drink of His goodness. Greg and Nancy Tankersley, y'all created an environment for a young, energetic, and fiery 26-year-old to learn to love, and showed me what it's like in Father's House. Steve Bremner, Jeremy Connor, and Hector Caban, each one of you have uniquely added to my life, particularly in the development of my writing. Scott Thompson, you showed me how to be authentic without being fake, burning through any circumstances in the path of life. Papa Leif, thanks for believing in me and showing me how to be a son.

Jeff and Wanda, you not only gave me Allessia, the greatest gift of my life, you also gave me a place in your family.

To my Mom, you are shining in eternity. I dearly miss you, but having seen what you're up to in Heaven, my heart is full in knowing the joy you now experience in the presence of Jesus. Louis, my brother, my friend. You are strong and noble.

Thank you to Todd Tyszka, Allessia Edwards, and the rest of the team who helped me with this edition of the book. Your contribution made this project possible. My prayer is that second edition of this book will be a timeless treasure and resource for all revivalists.

Thank you to the mothers, fathers, and friends in my life who endorsed this book: Leif Hetland, Jenn Stockman, Robert Gladstone, Scott Thompson, Keith Collins, Jon Potter, Scott Nary, and Peter Putnam.

I have so many friends to give thanks, gratitude, and honor to, that words and pages cannot capture or express. I love you all.

Finally, I would like to thank you, the reader. You've invested in me and I, in return, hope to invest in you with the contents of this book.

FOREWORD

When David and I met in Physical Science class in 1994, I thought he was a nice guy, but we ran in different circles, so for the first few years, we became more acquaintances than friends. I played volleyball and got good grades. He was a skateboarder with wild hair and a wild personality to match. We had the occasional class together, yet our worlds were far apart. My parents raised me in the church, and I grew up loving Jesus. Dave went to church from time-to-time but didn't have a grid for what a true relationship with God was like.

Everything changed during our junior year when Dave had a radical encounter with Jesus. His entire life flipped upside down. Dave was known for being a trickster and a troublemaker. So, when he met Jesus, the whole school took notice. Why am I telling you both of our stories? It's because it is just that, our story. What I realize now is that the Dave I met in 9th grade was searching for acceptance, love and purpose. It's hard to see when you don't really know who you are yourself and what you may have that others don't. The Dave of 11th grade was a totally transformed person who found love, acceptance, and purpose in Jesus.

He began attending the youth group at my church. He was a brand-new Christian; he didn't know the religious "rules," so he became just as wild for God. All he knew was that God changed his life, and he became hungry to experience as much of God as he could. He devoured the Word and every message that talked about the "more" of God. God consumed his entire life. He was never satisfied. Every time he saw a "burning bush," he would turn aside to see what God was doing and then go after it until it became his. I didn't realize it then, but the day David Edwards met Jesus was the day my life would forever change.

This story isn't about how we became a couple. We can save that for another book. It story is about David, a man after God's heart—a man so consumed with God that he changed the people around him, which is where I come in. As I said, I grew up in church, I knew God my entire life, but Dave showed me that there was always more of God to discover if I would go after Him. The fire in Dave's heart kindled the fire in my heart. Never again would I be satisfied if I didn't experience "more!"

We became a couple in 1998 after we graduated. Three years later, we were married. Having have been together 20 years now, what I can say about Dave is that the fire lit inside of him at 16 has NEVER burned low. The revivalist John Wesley says, "I set myself on fire, and people come to watch me burn." This quote describes who Dave is; he is a burning one.

More than a book, this is his life. Leif Hetland always says, "first you receive, then you become, and then you release." After stewarding his revelations and personal encounters for years, Dave is finally releasing the testimony of his life.

Psalm 25:14 says, "There is a private place reserved for the lovers of God, where they sit near him and receive the revelation-secrets of His promises." Dave has determined to live his life seated in the heavenly places, and *The Call for Revivalists* is the revelation-secrets of his life with God.

It is interesting to me how significant our given names are because they always seem to reveal the gold inside of us. Dave could have been given another name, in fact, he almost was, but something in the heart of his parents said, no, he is a David.

Often, as I read about the life of David in the Bible—his devotion, his battles, his love—I see similarities in my own Dave. Recently, when I was reading Psalms, Papa God began to show me something new. David may have been the most significant prophet of the Old Testament, yet he wasn't known primarily as a prophet. The Psalms give us the heart of Father God, show us the life of Jesus, and reveal the creative breath of Holy Spirit. It's unlike any book in the Bible, and dare I say, it is the most quoted and read book of the Bible. Why? Because David tapped into the Father's heart and gave feelings to whom the Godhead is. He was a New Testament prophet in an Old Covenant world. He prophesied unforeseen revelations in the Father's heart.

My Dave has also lived his life this way. He too has tapped into the Father's heart and been entrusted with revelation-secrets. You may think I say this because I am his wife. No, I say this because it is the truth. I was talking to some of our closest friends this morning, and I asked, "Who would you say Dave is?" Having seen both the best and the worst of us, their response brought me to tears. I hope their words allow you to capture the heart of a man who has poured his life into this book:

> I believe Dave is one of the greatest prophets of our
> generation. He is able to translate the blueprints he
> receives in Heaven and make them accessible here. He is
> otherworldly, cosmic in thought—not limited by what is
> seen, felt, or heard on Earth. He looks into the expanse
> of creation, sees what God is doing, and hears what He is
> saying. Even with his gaze on the cosmos, he still sees

the shy girl in the corner, listening to Papa's thoughts over her. He holds the heart of those in front of him very close, making him a man after God's heart.

Dave originally wrote this book in 2012; it was a dream in his heart that I whole-heartedly supported. It has taken him four years to re-write it, but wow, now I can say it was worth the wait. I have walked beside him on this journey of becoming who God has called us to be and the Heavenly Family that we belong to, which was a catalyst for the book to reach its full potential. As I read through it again last week, I saw the book for what it truly is—a prophetic word to this generation. It's sure to provoke you to jealousy in the best kind of way. Kingdom Family is for everyone, and this book is your invitation. When you taste and see that He is good, you too will encounter Him and become a burning one, a revivalist.

Dave, I am beyond proud of you. It is the absolute honor and joy of my life to walk beside you as your partner. You are known in Heaven, but I believe you will be remembered on Earth as one completely consumed, always expecting the miraculous, and recklessly driven by Love. You are a revivalist! David, my beloved, I am well pleased with you.

ALLESSIA EDWARDS
Partner Director, Global Mission Awareness
Proud Wife

INTRO

HEAVEN ON EARTH

THE **MANIFESTATION** OF **HEAVEN** ON **EARTH**⋯

...is the vision that drives my life. I am burning to see it realized in my generation. I am daily transformed by my pursuit to experience the presence of God revive the cosmos. The Father's plan for creation has always been Family—a place where everyone feels at home and finds where they belong.

HEAVENLY FAMILY REVIVES THE **COSMOS** TO **GOD'S ORIGINAL DESIGN.**

When we discover our place in the Family, we become revivalists. Revivalists are those who see the Earth from Heaven's perspective and revive the Earth according to God's design. The members of the Family are supernatural sons and daughters of God. They can do the impossible, believe the incredible, and encounter the majesty of Heaven on Earth.

15

Jesus says in Luke 12:49 that He "longs to cast fire on the Earth." The fire of the Spirit can only come through those born of the Spirit, who are revived themselves. When the fire touches them, they become the fire. Likewise, when the fire touches us, this is who we become.

WE ARE THE **FIRE! HE** IS **SENDING US** TO **IGNITE** THE **EARTH.**

"Revivals" and "revivalists" are arising in this hour at an unprecedented pace. Places like Bethel Church in Redding, California promote revival cultures all over the world. This approach mirrors the ministry of John Wesley, who would not only preach the good news of Jesus, but also plant "revival centers" in cities touched by the revival, keeping the movement aflame. People were brought into the Kingdom, discipled, then sent out to carry the torch of revival to the surrounding areas. His community approach to ministry produced The Great Awakenings—a revival movement that endured from one century to the next. The lasting effects of the revival are still felt today. I have studied revivals and revivalists for over twenty years, and I believe we are in a "time such as this."

WE HAVE THE **OPPORTUNITY** TO **SEE** A **WORLDWIDE REVIVAL**
THAT WILL **ECLIPSE** EVEN **THE GREAT AWAKENINGS.**

ALL CREATION

I would characterize a revivalist as one whose heart has been touched by Heaven to such a degree that they long to see moves of God among people, in cities and nations, and across all creation.

For the anxious longing of the creation waits eagerly for the revealing of the sons of God.

Romans 8:19 NASB

The sons and daughters of God are revivalists. The world is waiting for those who can show them the Father. Everyone longs to belong and longs to be part of a family. Humanity groans the for supernatural ones to answer the cry in their heart to find their true home.

Jesus died for our sins, rose again for our salvations, and ascended to make us heirs of His Spirit. The ascension is essential because it activated the sending of the Holy Spirit. When we are filled with the Spirit, we are transformed into the image of Jesus. The Baptism of the Spirit is significant and vital to our lives and unlocks our true heavenly form.

IT IS A **METAMORPHOSIS** THAT TAKES **US** FROM **LIVING NATURAL** LIVES TO **LIVING SUPERNATURAL LIVES**, FROM **NATURAL** BEINGS TO **SUPERNATURAL BEINGS.**

Once we realize who we are in God and the "surpassing greatness of power towards us who believe," we reach the place where we are ready to begin. The church in the first century demonstrated life in the Spirit, which is why they were so powerful. Tragically, much of Christianity today has replaced power with doctrine. The world does not need more doctrine. What they need is a demonstration of the Spirit and power. The church needs a supernatural theology that meets their needs. Many in the church desire to return to the first century. That was two thousand years ago. My vision is that we as the church would not go back, but move forward, honoring their experience by flying higher and going further than they ever imagined.

The theme of this book is to activate a supernatural lifestyle. When sons and daughters take their seat at the Family Table as Heirs of Heaven on Earth, this becomes a reality. The Heavenly Family believes that their Father can do anything.

FAMILY IS THE SETTING FOR HEAVEN ON EARTH AND CREATES A CULTURE WHERE THE SUPERNATURAL IS NATURAL.

The revelations, stories, testimonies, and encounters I share with you in this book are an invitation for you to find your place in the Family and experience God in new, creative, and supernatural ways.

I have tasted and seen some tremendous things in God, but I know there is so much more. Journey with me as I share with you both my experiences and my dreams of what I feel God is doing in our generation and generations to come.

WRITE THE VISION

> And the Lord answered me: 'Write the vision; make it plain on tablets, so he may run who reads it.
>
> Habakkuk 2:2 ESV

This verse has a special place in my history with God. Bobby Conner and Larry Tomczak, two pioneers of supernatural Christianity, have both prophesied it over my life. It has inspired me to express my relationship with God through writing. My aim as I write is to encourage you to run. I do not desire to write a book full of activities to get you excited, but to set you on fire. If it's not sent from Heaven, then Heaven's culture will not be present. If Heaven is present, then the Spirit will leap within you and activate a supernatural lifestyle.

SPARKS OF REVIVAL WILL COMBUST WITHIN YOU, CONNECTING YOU TO THE HEART OF JESUS.

My prayerful declaration for this book is to cause you to encounter God. You will reach out and touch Him on a new level. What you discover you will become, and the radiance of He who sits on the throne in Heaven will be present in your life. You will shine on those around you, causing them to burn and experience God in His love and power.

I began writing my experiences with God and the things he spoke to me through his Word almost immediately after I was born again. This practice has continued to this day. Upon writing this book, I went back to read what he had shown me and found patterns of revelation. They connected to each other like puzzle pieces. Next, I noticed it fanned out into my life experiences. The content of messages I heard from leaders and the daily interactions I had with my friends all tied into the revelation God was showing me. I would step back every so often to look up at this beautiful mural God was painting in my life. The amazing thing is that He was orchestrating everything to line-up with the vision at just the right time. Ten years ago the book would have been radically different than it is now. Ten years from now, the same could be said. Hopefully, the snapshot I get to share with you here will build up your faith, set you on fire, and bring you closer to Him.

Another prophetic word given to me by Bobby Conner was that I had the "pen of a ready writer." It was a call to be prepared to write the visions as they would come. The Sons of Issachar understood the times and the seasons, and they knew what Israel should do. I think this is the essence of a prophetic life and prophetic literature. The release of the message is at just the right juncture in history suitable to its fulfillment. It is like a gear plate inside a transmission that is needed to get the vehicle to operate at higher RPMs. Through this book, I can connect with you and transmit the things God has deposited in my life.

IN READING IT, MAY YOU RUN!

PREFACE

MY REVIVAL HISTORY

BROWNSVILLE

I was privileged to be part of the Brownsville Revival in Pensacola, FL, which began in 1995 and continued into the first few years of the new millennium. Over two million people gave their lives to Jesus in this revival, many of them filled with the Spirit. Two prevailing themes of the revival were repentance and presence. The presence of God was so "thick" that visitors would go back to their home churches and discover that the same presence at the revival had accompanied them. As a result, small pockets of revival popped up all over the US and even around the world. The church at large felt the impact. Worship moved from hymnal based into expression based, and God's presence became more accepted.

I made my first trip to Brownsville in 1998, at the age of 18. I was saved the year before, just a couple months before my 17th birthday. My friends and I were extremely hungry for God and went to Brownsville to satisfy this appetite.

We arrived at our first service a little late and had to sit in the overflow building during the message. I sat on the edge of my seat, full of anticipation, as Evangelist Steve Hill preached the Gospel.

I HAD THE **FAITH** OF A **LITTLE CHILD** AS I WAITED TO **EXPERIENCE GOD MOVE** IN **AMAZING WAYS.**

After the message, we walked over to the main building to watch the prayer time. At each service, the leaders would pray for everyone who wanted a touch from God, but our group thought that the prayer time was just for those who responded to the call for salvation, so we unintentionally missed-out. However, we still experienced God's presence. We stood in the back section of the sanctuary and observed as God touched people so powerfully they could not stand. Suddenly, my knees began to buckle and shake. Luckily, I was leaning on the wall of the sound booth, enabling me to catch myself before hitting the floor.

SOMETHING CAME FROM **BEHIND ME** THAT **FELT** LIKE **WATER** AND **WIND.**

I turned around to see what was happening and caught a glimpse of Pastor John Kilpatrick was walking across the back of the auditorium laying hands on people. He was moving at a pretty swift pace, so almost as soon as I looked, he was already on the other side of the building. The presence lessened in intensity the further away he got from me. The most impressive thing to me about that experience was that when he walked by me he was at least 20 feet away and the presence of God was such that I could not stand. Plus, it was as if he moved in a vortex of the water and wind of the Spirit.

Vision, desire, and destiny filled my heart. How did he find such an extravagant place in God? I wanted that. I wanted to know how to have a relationship with God like him.

"How could I walk in God's presence like this?"

"How could I become a carrier of revival?"

"What is the secret to becoming a revivalist?"

Thoughts like these daily filled my mind after that inaugural trip to the Revival. Over the next year, my hunger continued to intensify. So, I went back the following summer to attend a men's conference and had even greater encounters with God. In fact, it was such a wonderful few days that I decided to attend their ministry school—Brownsville Revival School of Ministry (BRSM). I thought, "If this was this intense for a week, what would it be like to live in this environment?" My close friend, Damian McCrink had already completed a year at the school and helped me settle into Pensacola.

I came for what I had experienced at the church, but what was happening at the school was even more intense. I began to learn so much on impacting the Earth with the power of God with a new level of understanding. There was a teacher there by the name of Dr. Robert Gladstone. He was a young man at the time, yet carried immense revelation. He taught the Bible with power, causing it to come alive. Yes, it was already alive to me, but now it was on steroids.

THE STORIES IN THE BIBLE THAT SEEMED LIKE FAIRY TALES SUDDENLY BECAME POSSIBLE.

One of the classes he taught during my first semester was about how we were the generation that would emerge to fulfill the call of God to the earth. When I heard this, my paradigm of what I thought would happen in the future began to shift with light. "Maybes" were translated into realities.

REVOLUTION

During my second semester, school President, Dr. Michael Brown, wrote a book on the theme of *Revolution*, which he released at The Call DC. This event was a gathering by Lou Engle of over 400,000 people on the National Mall to fast and pray to turn the nation back to God. The release of the book was designed to inspire the young people to join the Jesus Revolution.

"Revolution" became our message and our life-blood. We were revolutionaries. As Dr. Gladstone illustrates:

"WHEN WE BUILD A HOUSE AND GOD COMES TO VISIT, THAT'S REVIVAL. WHEN GOD BUILDS THE HOUSE AND THEN COMES TO LIVE IN IT, THAT'S REVOLUTION!"

What happens to society when true revival hits? It doesn't just have an impact on the church. It impacts the world. Revolution is when revival breaks out of the four walls of the church and society itself feels the influence. This concept was revolutionary for us at the time. So, to

24

observe the impact on global spirituality in the twenty years since has been astounding.

I transferred to the new FIRE School of Ministry in between my second and third semesters, launched by Dr. Brown and other BRSM faculty. (FIRE is an acronym for Fellowship for International Revival and Evangelism.) The New Jesus Revolution was already our prime focus, so when FIRE began, the message burned in us on a new level. However, I quickly realized that if one of the revelations of revival is to become a revolution, then a lifestyle of revival must drive the revolution. You're a revivalist if revival characterizes your life. And revival to me, in grandiose simplicity, is the life in Heaven giving life to the Earth.

HEAVEN ON EARTH IS REVOLUTIONARY

It is God taking back His place in the hearts of his children. When He is with His kids—you and me—He is where He has always wanted to be.

My second year of school, circa 2001, was amazing. We were using then innovative words like "apostolic," and "community." The seeds of which were laying a foundation for my walk with God and my writing in the coming years. In my "Preaching and Public Speaking Class," we had two assignments. One was a topical sermon, and one was an exegetical sermon. Before this class, I had only shared brief devotions with people, but never preached. I was excited and took the assignments seriously.

First up was the topical sermon and I decided to do it on the verse I mentioned earlier, Romans 8:19. I titled the message, "The Revelation of the Sons of God." It was an orator based sermon, which meant it needed an introduction, three points, a conclusion, and an altar call. I was also

25

studying Daniel at the time, so the premise of the message was the revealing of Daniel as a son of God in the court of King Nebuchadnezzar.

Next, I titled the exegetical sermon, "The Sword and the Stone." It was about David defeating Goliath by choosing to fight with a stone rather than a sword. I even had a toy sword hidden, ready to pull it out just at the right moment of my speech to illustrate the point. [Years later, as I was writing this book, a young lady gave me a prophetic word that included a reference to the movie, *The Sword and the Stone*. God will send us messages like this to confirm that we are on his path.]

These two "assignments" merged into the central message of my life for the next decade. Everything God showed me, even what I heard from others, all seemed to filter through my brain and spirit into this message. And through the years God has sharpened it and settled it into my heart. The seeds of those messages have become the foundation for this book.

The time I spent at BRSM and FIRE introduced me to one of the biggest revivals that the world has ever seen and my first glimpse at those who wanted to revolutionize society.

A BURNING FIRE

I love to journal the things God speaks to me. Sometimes I write for hours, devouring pages and pages. I would become so shocked, touched, enlightened, and moved by the things that He showed me that it became like an intense fire burning within me. Often, I would shut the book and cover my ears because it was too much to process. The revelation just kept coming and coming. It was almost overbearing. I wanted to share what He was showing me with people "so bad." I had no platform, no ministry. It was just He and I. My only ministry was to the page, and I was entrusted to steward and record what he was showing me. I understood Jeremiah's heart when he exclaimed:

> If I say, 'I will not mention Him, or speak any more in His name,' there is in my heart as it were a burning fire shut up in my bones, and I am weary of holding it in, and I cannot.

vv 20:9

I said, "Lord what are you doing to me?" His answer revealed that He was allowing the word to burn deep inside of me. It was burning up everything so that the word was all that was left. It was not just to be knowledge or information. The word was to become me, and I was to become the word. I would, when the time came, not just be sharing something I learned, but I would be sharing what I had become. It was now a part of my being.

When His word swirls in you like this, He is all that is left. You don't lose your personality, but every part of your personality becomes immersed in the message and transformed by his voice. An environment is created inside of you that gives power to your words. When you communicate them, they will resonate in the hearts of those who hear because God has spoken through you.

He was also shaking me on the inside so that when I spoke, my words would shake things on the outside. I would write with fire and passion born from experience, not just from knowledge and intellect.

In the early years of my preaching and writing, I would pray or say something along these lines, "Lord, let every word that is of you bear fruit and every word I speak that is not of you fall to the ground." I changed my view on that later as I concluded that God could recreate our words and their intentions as we speak them when our words flow from intimacy with Him. He will bring life to what we say.

My goal is for the mysteries of Heaven to become realities here on the Earth and to raise up a supernatural generation. I have been blogging along these lines since 2006 and have finally come to a place to compile what I believe will be a manual for a generation to walk in a revival that produces a supernatural revolution. We will journey through the call for supernatural sons and daughters to arise and join with their mothers and fathers to shake the Earth.

THE REVIVALIST'S ANTHEM

The **Awakening** of a **Generation**
The **Emergence** of the **Supernatural**
The **Sound** of **Revival**
Jesus said **They** would do **Greater Works**
This is their **Mantle**
This is their **Call**
With **Fire** in their **Eyes**, they will **Outshine** the **Stars**
And **Outburn** the **Sun**
They are **Not Found Hiding** when the **Giants Come**
They will Rise
They will Fight
They will **Free** their **Generation**
Heaven is the **Anthem** that **Burns** in their **Hearts**
Signs, Wonders, Miracles, set them **Apart**
Calling a **Generation** to **Reform** and **Revive**
They will **Change** a **Nation** because **Jesus** is **Alive**
Rise Mothers
Rise Daughters
Rise Fathers
Rise Sons
Rise Revivalists

ONE

SUPERNATURAL QUEST

"**WHAT** DOES IT **LOOK LIKE** WHEN **HEAVEN** COMES **DOWN**?"

Deep into worship at a youth conference, our hearts were crying out for the answer to the question asked by this popular Bethel Music song. My heart was burning with the reality of Heaven moving in our midst. The young men and women all around me fully engaged as the sounds of life flowed from their lips. We were ripe for a visitation, pulling the strings of God's heart. How could He resist us? He wanted to show Himself to us more than we desired for Him to come.

"It looks like you," is the answer God roared back to me. His response caused an internal explosion in my spirit. I realized that Heaven was aware of what was happening. A seemingly small meeting of youth on a Florida beach had God's full attention.

I knew I had to navigate the youth to connect with God's response. He wanted them to "taste and see" Heaven. As I was thinking about these things, the Youth Pastor, Chris Oliver, handed me the microphone to share what was on my heart, unaware of the download I just received. It was a divine set up as both of us were simply flowing in the Spirit.

I took the song lyrics and aimed them at everyone in the room, asking, "What does it look like when Heaven comes down?" I then shared God's answer, "It looks like you." Next, I instructed them to become the answer themselves and declare, "It looks like me!" They followed my lead with precision, and together they said, "It looks like me!" They started to feel it, so I urged them to say it again. "It looks like me," they shouted.

Moving them into the moment, I increased my intensity as I implored, "Now say it and mean it." Then they cried out, "It Looks Like Me," as their voices rose. Now, they were capturing the moment as I was.

Energized, I lifted my voice to the top of its capacity, "Now say it with everything that is in you, with all your heart, and all that you want to see God do in your generation." "What does it look like when Heaven comes down?" As I called out, "It looks like me," they erupted like volcanoes of furious love and called back, "IT LOOKS LIKE ME!"

Their voices were given to release the sound emerging within them. The sound that was always there. They were born with it. All that was needed was a mother or a father to show them where it was and how to bring it to the surface.

What was taking place? God was capturing the heart of a generation. When Elijah had prepared the sacrifice on Mt. Carmel, it created an expectation among the people that God was about to move. The fuel had been poured out on their hearts, waiting to ignite with the flames of Heaven.

> And at the time of the offering of oblation, Elijah the prophet came near and said, 'O Lord, God of Abraham, Isaac, and Israel, let it be known this day that You are God in Israel... Answer me O Lord, that this people may know the You O Lord are God, and that You have turned their hearts back. Then the fire of the Lord fell and consumed the burnt offering.

> 1 Kings 18:36a-37 ESV

Often, God will take us through a progression, whether in a public meeting or in our prayer closets that make us a suitable offering—preparing our hearts to receive more of his fire. Our progression was to realize that we were the answer, we were what it looked like for Heaven to come down.

Chris, synced with God's heart, began praying for the fire of Heaven to fall as he motioned for the leaders to lay hands on the young people. We found ourselves thrown on the altar that day. God did what He always does in environments like this; He poured His fire on us. The presence of God was so intense as the leaders prayed for the kids that many were unable to stand. All of us could feel the atmosphere transform as Heaven came down. Youth and adults alike were lying all over the floor basking in the weight of the glory, intoxicated by His presence.

SOME **SHOOK** AND **VIBRATED** AS IF **THEY** WERE
SHOCKED BY **ELECTRICITY.**

Others were laughing or crying as God touched each person right where they were at in life. Many were baptized in the Holy Spirit and began to speak in heavenly languages. Others began to experience deliverance from demons. Likewise, those dealing with pain, physical ailments, and depression were touched, healed, and set free.

After about an hour, the students began praying for each other, releasing another—more powerful—wave of God's presence. Those just recovering from the first one took a surprise hit from the second. The leaders began to take a step back and watch the wonderful presence of God as he touched the youth. A couple more hours passed as we soaked up Heaven.

We moved beyond intellectual Christianity and opened the door of experiential Christianity. The lyrics we sang in the song actually happened to us. Our words weren't empty; rather, they made contact in heavenly places. Singing about Heaven coming down caused Heaven to come down.

The fire fell and burned in the hearts of kids that day. As I think about the stories I've read about in church history of revival breaking out, this experience seems to be just as powerful, if not more, as many of them. Of the ones in attendance that day, most are still burning brightly for Jesus years after this transforming encounter.

THE BIBLE IS SUPERNATURAL

The blueprint given in the Bible is one where supernatural moves of God are normal, not the exception. The Bible itself is a collection of encounters, like the one above, designed to guide us to experience the wonderful stories it contains for our own lives. It inspires us to discover the God we read about and get to know Him for ourselves. His desire is for us to encounter Him in the same ways as our Biblical heroes and heroines. Their stories are runways for us to fly into the sky of the miraculous and enjoy even more wondrous adventures than they experienced.

Many people, both in the church and in the world, think of the Bible as either fiction, purely metaphorical, or merely a book from which to glean. The stories in the Bible seem so incredibly supernatural and so far beyond anything we encounter in our everyday lives that it is hard to believe the things written on its pages are attainable in our lives.

Many leaders, pastors, teachers, and scholars teach that supernatural encounters have either passed away or reserved for a futuristic age. Known as Cessationism, this type of theology doesn't leave a lot of room for experience. Much of this is unintentional because a majority of Westernized Christianity has viewed their faith through the perspective of "logic and reason." The unfortunate side-effect has left even Christian leaders with a perception that they are stuck in the middle of two supernatural eras. Kingdom Theology suggests that the Bible hasn't replaced the supernatural; it's the gateway to the supernatural.

The entire Bible is a supernatural tale of God and humanity. It stands as a guide for us to become supernatural and to activate our heavenly inheritance as sons and daughters of God. It is a Superhero Training Manual. To remove the supernatural element from the Word is to erase the need for it. If we do this, then we might as well throw it away. What good is it if it does not stand out from every other book ever written as truly divine? The reason it is so powerful is that it introduces us to a

35

relationship with Jesus. The life He lived on the Earth was one full of the Holy Spirit, demonstrating the power, love, and wisdom of the Father everywhere He went. We read the Bible to become like Him. His Spirit speaks to us and guides through the Word. The same heroics we read about are intended to become testimonies that fill our own lives. These stories are real, written not so we can read about the things God used to do, but so we can read about what God desires to do today.

THE **BIBLE** IS A **BOOK OF MIRACLES** THAT **SHOWS US HOW** TO **BECOME MIRACLES.**

Our lives should demonstrate that the Bible is nonfiction because our lives are a demonstration of the power in the Bible.

> And when I came to you brethren, I did not come with superiority of speech or of wisdom, proclaiming to you the testimony of God. For I determined to know nothing among you except Jesus Christ, and Him crucified. I was with you in weakness and in fear and in much trembling, and my message and my words were not in persuasive words of wisdom, but in demonstration of the Spirit and of power, so that your faith would not rest on the wisdom of men, but on the power of God.
>
> 1 Corinthians 2:1-5 NASB

To know and experience God while here on Earth is what I believe everyone longs for in the depths of their being. The need to fill the space inside of them, which was created to capture and release God's love, is what gives them over to any of the causes or beliefs that occupy their lives. The need to fill the void becomes a quest for meaning that can only

36

find true satisfaction in God Himself. Everyone on Earth has an internally programed desire to return to the Family of God. Encounters turn into lifestyle when everyone discovers their place at the Father's table.

> He is the image of the invisible God, the firstborn of all
> creation.

> Colossians 1:15 ESV

God did not just manufacture a new product in the creation of the human race, He modeled us after His Son. We are created in the image of God. "Image" refers to an imprint. He imprinted Himself into the fabric of the Earth then breathed the substance of His Being into the shape made from His Form, resulting in the animation of Adam. We are more than just a look-a-like. Humanity itself is a cast, an exact recreation of God's own Son. Because of this, there is in the heart of mankind, a longing to experience something supernatural, something more, something above and beyond all the natural life has to offer. Perfection, completion, and union are found in Him.

JESUS IS THE EXPRESSED PERSONIFICATION OF HEAVEN ON EARTH AND THE ANSWERED CRY OF ALL CREATION.

He is the essence of our true identity and sonship. To know Him is to know God. Creation longs to know Creator. The secret of creation resides in Him. He is the key to filling the need of humanity. He is the mystery of the riddle of life.

The story of the Bible is the story of Jesus. From Genesis to Revelation, He is revealed as the Key, the restorer of His Father's Family.

The Bible is a two-dimensional blueprint of a three-dimensional Person—Jesus—who, as Michal Koulianous says, "lives in its pages." If we take the supernatural out of the Bible, we remove the essence of Jesus.

FILLING THE EARTHLY WITH THE HEAVENLY

The earthly life of Jesus was heavenly, full of all kinds of supernatural activity including signs, wonders, and miracles. A true representation of Heaven will preserve Heaven's characteristics. If we are His image in the Earth, we will live heavenly, supernatural lives as well.

The origin of a supernatural life is found in intimacy. Intimacy fulfills the heart's cry for union with its Creator and generates an atmosphere of the miraculous. If the supernatural is missing, then life will be unfulfilled because the intimate longing of the soul will be unsatisfied.

Sadly, many live with the misguided belief that they have to die to experience something heavenly. However, Jesus is the entrance to Heaven, not death. Through our relationship with Him, we can enjoy Heaven now. Those who don't know Him are looking for fulfillment, purpose, and destiny in their lives. The image of God is in them as a driving force to take hold of the supernatural. And all too often, it is found in things the world has to offer, rather than in the presence, power, and the love of God. If there is a theology in place that suggests that the supernatural has passed away, then true fulfillment in life will never be realized. We are created to be naturally supernatural.

HEROICS

I love to watch sports. My favorite is soccer. To watch an amazing run, pass, or shot on goal is enthralling. I love to watch the matches, cups, and championships. I even love the off-season, including the transfers of players and how the teams strategize for the coming year.

What is your favorite sport? Why is it so entertaining? For many, it surpasses the game and becomes part of the way they live their lives. When we watch sports played by men and women gifted with great natural talent, we are elated and thrilled. It takes us beyond ourselves. We admire those who can accomplish things that we cannot. We fantasize about being them. When they win, we are on the moon, but when they lose, it makes us feel as if we have also failed. Whatever we give our hearts to will be revealed in a season of failure. If we view even sports through our relationship with Jesus, then even in failure, we can enjoy it without being overcome by it.

I love to read as well. Our society is shifting with technology as other forms of media now offer an escape, but there is nothing like reading a book and allowing our imagination to visualize the story.

The quest for the supernatural reveals why books with this theme are so popular. Why is Harry Potter is so captivating? It provides supernatural release. Many love the series because of how it makes them feel without realizing the origin of some of the dark themes it contains. What about Lord of the Rings and The Chronicles of Narnia, which are Christian allegories? They are written to explore worlds where the supernatural is real. They have been bestsellers among believers and unbelievers for generations because they supply satisfaction to something that burns deep within us. The Source of true supernatural experience is Jesus. He is the "wardrobe" everyone longs to walk through to discover their true supernatural existence.

Cinema is another outlet for the supernatural. We are privileged to live in an age where we can literally watch someone else's imagination on the screen. Why does our culture have such an appetite for movies, movie stars, and television shows? Some of the biggest movies as of late have been about superheroes such as *The Avengers, X-Men,* and *Wonder Woman.* Could it be that there is something inside of us the cries out, "I am created to be like them?" No one dreams of being a wimp. Everyone wants to be the hero.

HEROISM IS IN OUR DNA.

Our bodies are designed to be conduits for the supernatural. Jesus is the ultimate superhero. We are drawn to Him because He reveals what it was like to be a superhero to a generation. Why does creation groan of the sons and daughters to be revealed? They long for actual superheroes—to be part of a Supernatural Family.

One time a Christian friend of mine stated that his hero was Superman because he had always wanted to fly. Superman is a legend, chief of all the superheroes and heroines. Why is a Christian's hero Superman? When we think about flying, Superman is usually the "go-to" person in our minds. There is a longing within us to be free even from the natural elements. We long to overcome natural problems and obstacles and to enjoy creation to the degree that would only be possible with supernatural ability. Flying would indeed be one of these abilities.

How many of us dreamed of flying when we were younger? I know I did. Somehow, as we grow older, dreams of flight get replaced by dreams of success. Flying becomes a metaphor instead of something to be realized. Yet, even as older and wiser ones, we still identify with Superman. I think there is a little bit of the spirit of Superman in all of us.

I am inspired when I watch a superhero movie because I know that God has created me to be more supernatural than these fictional heroes could ever be. I am on a supernatural quest. I long to see a supernatural generation arise. May these movies and books no longer be substitutes, rather, catalysts that edge us closer to realizing who we are as sons and daughters of God in the Earth. We should not have to look at fictional characters to find an example of that which is supernatural. We should be able to find super men and women within the church, within ourselves! In Christ, we have been born into the Supernatural Family. We are heavenly beings walking the Earth. We are Super Men! We are Wonder Women!

SUPERNATURAL QUESTION

If no one meets the supernatural need, those who are searching for it are left feeling empty. Then they are susceptible to the influence of counterfeit supernatural power such as false religions, cults, and witchcraft. All creation longs for the supernatural experience, and they will do anything to find it. They will kill, wage war, and even fly airplanes into buildings. They consult mediums, wizards, psychics, pornography, sadistic poverty, and perverted wealth. This desire increases when there is no supernatural theology within the church. The world is missing supernatural inspiration, and they are looking everywhere to find it. They are asking the same question we were at the youth conference: "What does it look like when Heaven comes down?"

SUPERNATURAL ANSWER

It looks like us! We are the ones who hold the keys to the supernatural. We are the ones who have true supernatural wisdom. We are the ones who show the supernatural way and demonstrate true supernatural power. Jesus is the only God in all of history who became a man—showing us the way to God and giving us the same supernatural power he possesses.

Creation needs us to be supernatural. Creation needs Jesus, and Jesus lives inside us. His passion is to reveal Himself through us. Through His people—His sons and daughters, mothers and fathers, brothers and sisters—He demonstrates to the world that He is Lord. It's a Family thing!

> For the anxious longing of the creation waits eagerly for
> the revealing of the sons of God.
>
> Romans 8:19 NASB

We must capture a supernatural vision in our lives. All creation groans for our revealing. We are the ones who know God. We are called to show them the way to God, which ultimately will fulfill the supernatural desires in their hearts.

> For the creation was subjected to futility, not willingly,
> but because of him who subjected it, in hope, that the
> creation itself will be set free from its bondage to

corruption and obtain the freedom of the glory of the children of God.

Romans8:20-20 ESV

All of Creation is looking for God so they can be set free from bondage. We must, as the Body of Christ, become Jesus to the world. We are the ones who know Him and are the only ones who can show them the way to everlasting life and spiritual fulfillment. Jesus can do anything, and he chooses to use us to accomplish his eternal missions. We are the superheroes they long for. We have supernatural abilities. He answers their cry through us.

I feel that as the church, we have merely "scratched the surface" of all that is available in God. I am introducing the concept of the supernatural here, but as we continue, you will find that it is limitless. God is limitless; there is no-thing He cannot do. If He resides in us, we become limitless as well.

My good friend Brandon has had a reoccurring dream in which he is able to swim underwater and breathe. Then he is able to come up out of the water and fly through the air. After flying around, he dives back into the water and swims around again. Ah, if words could capture such a picture of all God has for us. Dreams are given to awaken our true identities in God. Brandon was given the dream to expand his awareness of how much more he can enjoy creation in a supernatural state.

We are the fulfillment of the supernatural desires that burn in the creation. The question mark for the world is to find out the meaning of life. The answer is simply this: "Christ in us, the hope of Glory," (Colossians 1:27). We are what it looks like when Heaven comes down.

The young people at the retreat received a glimpse of the power of God, which lit a fire in the secret place of their hearts. True passion, energy, and life began to surface like a spring from this place. Jesus met their supernatural need. By default, He has become their Source. They will not need to drink from that which supplies counterfeit supernatural fulfillment. In drinking from the Source, Jesus springs up a well in them (John 4), making them the source of the Source.

SUPERNATURAL SPLENDOR

The world becomes aware of the answer to the question as we reveal our place in God's Family. When we heal their sick and raise their dead, the "light bulb" of illumination will shine in their spirits, breaking away the spiritual bondage that clings to their hearts. Our supernatural hearts do not beat until the defibrillator of revelation shocks us, sparking the electric pulse of the life of the Spirit. The world needs this spark, this quickening. The world and the church need models of supernatural splendor who display the power of Jesus wherever they go. They need those whose supernatural hearts are beating to show them how to become alive. They need revival. They need revivalists. This is the Call for Revivalists!

SAILING THE SUPERNATURAL SEAS

The church itself is like a great ship stuck inside of a bottle. The belief system that writes of the supernatural experience for another age keeps the church trapped by her own way of thinking. There is a way out—a smashing of the bottle and christening of the voyage. The church is the vessel built to endure the storms and bring peace to every vestige of life.

"It is safe inside the bottle," so we think, even though is nothing more than shattering glass. We must activate our faith in Jesus and push out into the deep. We cannot remain hidden!

A song lyric by the band, Dogwood, gives us language for navigating the seas: "Lord you're the Captain that I wish that I could be, and I will sail with you forevermore from this day forward." The One who builds the ship is the One who created the seas, and He knows how to handle them. Many are afraid of the supernatural because of simple lack of faith. Trust activates the supernatural in us.

> And behold a there arose a great storm on the sea, so the boat was being covered with the waves; but Jesus Himself was asleep. And they came to Him and woke Him saying, save us Lord we are perishing!" He says to them "Why are you afraid, you men of little faith?" Then He got up and rebuked the winds and the sea, and it became perfectly calm.
>
> The men were amazed, and said, "What kind of man is this, that even the winds and the sea obey Him?
>
> Matthew 8:24-27 NASB

"What kind of man is this?" Jesus could stand firm in the midst of a stormy sea. The natural scene reflected what was going on inside of both Jesus and his disciples, which is the reason why they had two different reactions to the situation. Jesus was at peace on the inside, which is why He was able to enforce peace on the outside. The disciples did not have the same peace of God on the inside as Jesus, which is why they were frightened by the chaos on the outside. At this moment, just like all creation, they needed a son of God to be revealed. And they just happened to have The Son of God in the boat with them. Jesus had faith because He had no storms on the inside. Therefore, He knew the storms on the outside would be easily overcome. If we are sons of God, then Jesus is always in the boat with us. Besides, what can the storms do, sink Jesus? We become unsinkable when we realize we are part of the Family.

SUPERNATURAL EXAMPLE

John G. Lake was a man known for wondrous miracles. I will share more about him in chapter six, but here is a quick introduction to the incredible display of power that flowed in his life.

One time, when he lived as a missionary in South Africa, he and his team were praying for a demon-possessed girl at a mental institution in Wales. All of the sudden, he was encircled in light, and in the next moment, he was flying through the air from South Africa to Wales. He cited certain landmarks along the way, even verifying them on a future journey. When he arrived at the institution, he went into the girl's room and cast out the demon. Instantly, he was back in South Africa.

On another occasion, after concluding a meeting with a local preacher, the man got up and flew out of the window. Others told him that the man was known as the "flying saint."

If this seems hard to believe, remember the Bible itself is composed of supernatural stories. If we struggle to believe these, then do we really believe the Scripture? The torch of the supernatural has been passed down throughout the generations. John G. Lake carried it in his generation, will you carry it in yours?

OTHERWORLDLY

Many of the superheroes in modern culture often come from other worlds. Their origin explains why they have so much supernatural power in our world. Jesus also came from another world—another realm, which explains His power. He not only came from another place, but He also came from the highest place. He not only has another power, but He also has the highest power.

Jesus came from Heaven to the Earth to empower us with all the power on His World—His Kingdom. When His disciples asked Him how to pray, He reveals to them that prayer is more than a transmission from one world to another. In "The Lord's Prayer," He shows them that prayer is the union of two worlds.

> Our Father in Heaven, hallowed be Your name, Your kingdom come, Your will be done, on earth as it is in heaven.

> Matthew 6:9-10 ESV

Jesus was not just giving something to repeat. In fact, the verse just before this warns against it. On the contrary, He gave a position of prayer, a new lifestyle, and a new way of being. He was revealing the secret of the supernatural, the secret to a culture of connecting two worlds—Heaven to Earth. Prayer itself is a union of God and man. When God comes, man ascends, leaping from their world to His, from their domain to His—the King's domain—Kingdom.

"Hallowed" which some translations update as "Holy" can also transliterate as "otherworldly." With this in view, it gives greater impact to the lines that follow it. A descriptive paraphrase might sound something like this:

> Our Father, King in the heavenly realm, Your name is set apart from the names on the Earth, it is otherworldly. You who dwell in another world, higher than ours, whose name is far above, and Whose Kingdom reigns supreme, let Your Kingdom in that world come to this world, and let the will of that world become the will of this world, and let it be done here as it is done there.

The plan for Jesus' coming was to reconnect these worlds permanently. This prayer was a description, illustration, and summarization of His life.

HEAVEN DESCENDS TO EARTH TO MAKE A WAY FOR EARTH TO ASCEND TO HEAVEN.

The fire we experienced at the youth service that night was a manifestation of this reality—a manifestation of Heaven on Earth.

This perspective of the Lord's Prayer is to be a lens through which to read the rest of the book and apprehend all that Heaven has to offer. I am calling us activate a supernatural lifestyle. I hope to help equip you in the art of revival. An army of revivalists is on the move and gaining strength as it advances the Kingdom of God all across the Earth.

ACTIVATION

Holiness is otherworldliness. Residing in Heaven while on the Earth is the life Jesus modeled. Take a few moments and pray through the Lord's Prayer with this perspective. Follow the example in the text, but use language that is personal to you. Allow Holy Spirit to enhance and develop your understanding of the prayer and the wisdom needed to apply it to your life. Take each stanza one day at a time with an emphasis on how you see your world that day. Write out everything God is showing you.

1. Our Father in Heaven

2. Hollowed (Otherworldy) is your name

3. Your Kingdom come

4. Your will be done

5. On Earth as it is in Heaven

DECLARATION

I resolve to become a supernatural son or daughter on the Earth. When Heaven comes down, it will look like me. My life will be a supernatural one—pursuing the power, presence, and love of Jesus. I am a revivalist!

RISE REVIVALISTS!

TWO

OUR PLACE IN THE SKY

WE WERE **CREATED** FOR **HEAVENLY ENCOUTNERS.**

To know and experience God is the purpose of our lives. Only in this place will we ever truly come alive. The Bible contains many fascinating encounters. We know about the heroes of the faith because of their incredible interaction with God. Their stories tell us that we can encounter God in ways that are designed just for us as well. When we encounter God, we become the encounter for those we influence to experience God. The Bible says that we are seated in heavenly places. It's time for us to take our place in the sky, and reveal the real Jesus to the Earth.

One of the most remarkable encounters of my life was a dream I had in 2001, which I refer to as the "Sky Dream." In the dream, I was sitting in a rock quarry. It had the shape of an amphitheater. There was a pool of water at the bottom. At the center, where the stage would have been, there was an open sky. People were people assembled all around me like I was sitting in a stadium. I was in the middle of the rock face, next to a booth that looked like something out of the *Flintstones*. Inside the booth was a teacher of mine from ministry school. Being prophetic, he represented the role of a prophet in the dream. He would phase or transfigure from himself, into Jesus, and then back again—repeatedly. To his left was my friend Brandon, who also had a friend to his left. Likewise, I had a friend sitting to my right. I knew these two were close friends, but ironically, I didn't know who they were, or at least, I had yet to meet them in the natural world.

The rock quarry and the people gathered together in it represented the church. There was an atmosphere of expectation all around us. It was as if we were all waiting for something. I kept looking to the prophet sitting in the booth to gauge the spiritual climate and how I should respond to it. Suddenly, to the right of the quarry, an enormous cloud drifted into frame. It had a dark-flat-blueish-gray tone. All-at-once, the feeling of fear arose within the church. I began to think about what clouds represent in Scripture. Immediately, my mind went to the glory cloud on Mt. Sinai and the glory filling King Solomon's temple. However, something didn't sit well with my spirit. It looked right, but it felt wrong. Many of the people began to freak-out, shouting "It is the Lord! Jesus is coming!" Their voices seemed to echo the feeling of fear that had accompanied the cloud.

Again, I looked to the prophet, who by now, had maintained the figure of the teacher, no longer phasing into and out of Jesus. There was a sharp look of concern coupled with agitation on his face. He remained silent. His silence, however, spoke louder to me than the explosions suspicious praises that were now floating around the amphitheater. His look confirmed what I felt on the inside. I joined him in silence, along with our friends, who also followed his lead. Others took notice and accompanied our protest.

The event was quite chaotic. Different people were responding in different ways, which seemed to coincide with where they were in life, their relationship with Jesus, and with those in attendance.

Next, the cloud moved from the right side of the sky to the left. As it shifted, it grew darker, scarier, and more intense. People followed it and began to amass on the left side at the top of the quarry, which was a high cliff. Confusion set in, and those closest to the edge fell off. We watched as they tumbled down into the water. Some also fell over the opposite edge. Those in the back of the crowd didn't see what was happening and continued to press forward. The ones penned up front began screaming when they realized they were about to be herded off the cliff. So many packed onto the rim that the ground started to break away. Pandemonium set in as the ground collapsed, spilling people in every direction.

The chaos snapped some of the people out of the delusion created by the cloud. Finally, they knew it wasn't Jesus, but an antichrist. Satan was disguising himself with something that appeared to be biblical. He clothed himself in a paradigm that many in the church viewed Jesus and the "end-times" through, and deceived them into missing the real Jesus. This negative worldview of eschatology and the goodness of God resulted in many falling away.

In the same moment, a second cloud appeared on the right side of the sky. This one was golden in with a bright light in the center of it. It was more like an expanse in the heavens than a cloud. The prophet began yelling, "Jesus is coming. Jesus is coming!" When the people connected to the prophecy, the cloud moved to the center of the sky, driving out the first cloud and the darkness it had cast over the left side of the quarry.

The center of the expanse was right in front of me now, bringing greater clarity and detail. It was massive and awesome. It seemed to be the very center of the universe and all existence. What I saw was much bigger than the Earth or the sky.

PEERING INTO A GREATER, ALL-ENCOMPASSING REALM, THE SIGHT BEFORE ME INTENSIFIED.

The more I was able to take in, the more it expanded. It was almost like a conversation. The more I ascertained, the more I was shown. The encounter itself was interacting with my level of absorption. Its appearance was dazzling. It sparkled and shimmered. There were golden tones throughout that seemed to be alive. The outer edge was a darker gold, rich and dense. It looked ancient, and I felt as if it contained the history of the universe. The closer I looked towards the center, the golden hue was much lighter and brighter. There were interworking's of gold and bright white, almost like a luminescent fabric that vibrated in waves of glistening life. The vibrations were heard in eternity past, present, and future—harmonizing all of space and time.

The feeling this cloud gave was seducing. I had to look, I had experience and behold what was before me. It drew me. I felt "more alive" than any other time in my life. As my eyes continued toward the center of the cloud, I knew what awaited me. It was a moment of unveiling. In order to look, my heart would be on full display. I didn't feel shame; rather, safety and comfort. I knew that in looking, my heart would be protected. I felt the awesomeness of the moment. There was a fear unlike the feeling produced by the first cloud. This fear was like the feeling on my wedding day, which culminates in the intimacy of oneness. It was blissful and intoxicating. It was the understanding that the destination of my sight was the center of the expanse, Who dwelled there, and the intimate union that gently waited for my gaze.

It was light outside as rays of sunshine replaced the shadows. The sun in its strength causes you to squint, even upon emerging from a brightly lit room. As I transferred my gaze from the sky to center of the cloud, I had the same sensation. The intensity of the light didn't burn my eyes. Although I had the natural instinct to shield them, there was no need because the light was accessible to my sight.

LIGHT INVITED ME TO LOOK AND **SEE.**

The entire array was an instantaneous interaction as my eyes accelerated toward the Source of the light—

JESUS HIMSELF, HOVERING IN THE MIDDLE OF THE **SKY, SHINING** LIKE A **SUPERNOVA**⋯

...in the golden expanse. He was so magnificently bright that I struggle to describe it. I had to fight to focus on his form through layers of white light that exuded from His being. To quickly glance upon Him was to see brilliance and whiteness. Gazing upon Him was like focusing on one of those three-dimensional pictures that you must look at intently to see the hidden image. Once you see it, the picture pops out. An endless countenance surrounded Him. There was more depth, texture, and reality inside of the expanse than on the outside. It was like peering into an eternal door. I gazed into true reality. In Him, I viewed everything—time, space, eternity—all at once.

I SAW A GLIMPSE OF ALPHA AND OMEGA.

Years after this dream, I continue to discover greater depth, details, and insight than ever before. It is as if the dream was a gift that I get to take with me the rest of my life, and every time I open it, there is something new and exciting never seen before. When I first had the dream, I had no words for the beauty of Jesus in the expanse. Now, when I recount the scene, it's as if I go back into the experience and take a look around at everything that was going on at that moment. To this day, words still fail to describe Jesus or recreate the weight of the impact of seeing Him in such a bright display. I cannot describe His form or His face. I still look intently at Him to find features in the midst of His radiance. It's like looking at the sun and trying to describe the surface to you—how the gases move, and solar flares jump here and there, or the collection of colors swirling around. I simply ask Jesus to take you into an encounter as you read this, so you too can experience the brightness of His countenance, shinning in His heavenly place.

As the cloud came to rest at the focal point in the sky, it captured the attention of the entire church.

ALL EYES WERE ON **JESUS.**

Each of us appeared to be engaged in our individual yet united encounters. We had a collective awareness. The time that passed from the appearing of the expanse to it moving to the sky's center was only a few seconds. Everything I have described occurred within those moments. As I stared at the Son, all earthly limitations faded away. I found myself right in front of the King of the Universe.

METAMORPHASIS

In the next moment, I was stunned as a flash of light sparked next to me. I watched in amazement as Brandon, like a rocket blasting-off, flew out into the center of the expanse and exploded into a massive fireball. It was like watching missile firing into the sun. As he flew, a trail of yellow light, like the tail of a comet, followed him. It looked like a fiery substance engulfed him with a white-hot interior. His destination was Jesus. He flew right into Him. In an instant, Brandon was hovering mid-air, slightly to the right of Jesus, just as moments before, he was sitting slightly to the left of the prophet. What I was watching happen in Heaven was mirroring what was happening on the Earth, forming a circle.

Encountering Jesus transfigured his appearance. His arms sprouted wings and were raised straight out on each side. He was glowing and awesome in appearance.

HE **LOOKED** LIKE A **HEAVENLY BEING**, YET **RETAINED** HIS **HUMANITY.**

It was a marriage of natural and supernatural, earthly and divine. There were layers of light around him, almost as if he was in a bubble of purity and light. He seemed to carry an environment around him, just as Jesus did when He appeared. Growth and expansion vibrated as he took his place in the sky as a son of God. True sonship is born in the presence of the Son. He looked over the Earth from his newfound heavenly seat with eyes to see as Heaven sees and a heart on fire with love.

All of this happened in a flash. During the dream, the details were imprinted in my mind like an x-ray while moving rapidly through the events. I was awestruck by his ascent. It released something inside of me at the speed of light. No sooner had he flown into the cloud before I felt something detonate inside me.

I FOUND MY IGNITION SKYWARD.

It was a rush of pure adrenaline. "I knew that I knew" I would make it. The question of flight, gravity, and natural law did not even cross my mind, nor did the thought of falling even occur to me. A storm of belief baptized my being. It was such a state of transcendence that my only viable response was to fly.

I may have had a taste of the array of emotions and faith Peter experienced just as he stepped onto the sea. The moment was irresistible. Peter saw with true sight, knowing it was safer on the water with Jesus than in the boat. Likewise, it was better for me to ride the clouds with Jesus than sitting on the rock face. There was no instruction manual. All I had to navigate was to follow Brandon's ascent. I was compelled to launch.

I LIT UP LIKE THE **MUSCHROOM CLOUD** OF A **NECLEAR EXPLOSION** AND **FLEW** INTO THE **EXPANSE**···

I **FLEW** INTO THE **REALM** OF **HEAVEN**···

I **FLEW** INTO THE VERY **PERSON** OF **JESUS**.

It was so quick, yet so expansive that the moment of impact is almost beyond articulation. I had an encounter with Jesus in which an explanation of this is beyond my ability to write. Instantly, I exploded into a fireball just like Brandon. Here we were, floating in the sky, with Heaven and Earth as our dwellings. I was on one side of Jesus, and Brandon was on the other. Again, similar to a few moments before when we were on either side of the prophet. Parallel. The natural scene is who we were in everyday life as part of the Body of Christ, but the supernatural scene is who we really are as part of the Heavenly Family.

The prophet represents the Ministry Gifts given to equip the church for the works of ministry in Ephesians 4:11. He phased into Jesus and back as a representation of the heavenly scene. An apostolic team flowing in fullness will have Jesus as their only agenda. They will recognize and prepare the church for His appearing. "The spirit of prophecy is the testimony of Jesus." Prophecy at this level pierces the heart with the perfection of Jesus. Our response was a true Jesus encounter.

Next, my peripheral vision expanded, and I could see all around. I was aware of the enormity and complexity of the situation. We were no longer viewing something "above and beyond" us. The encounter absorbed us, sucking us into the vacuum of irresistibility. We became characters in the movie. We were no longer viewing Heaven from Earth;

we were now viewing Earth from Heaven. "Above and beyond" became the here and now."

I had outstretched wings as well, yet I could still feel my hands. It was like a having both together, or one or the other, available as needed.

WAVES OF ELECTRICITY AND FIRE PULSATED THROUGHOUT MY BODY.

It was an awareness of life, unlike anything I have ever known. I knew I was alive before, but now I was alive in the fullness of union with Jesus.

My ascent became the catalyst for our two remaining friends to join us in the sky. I watched as they ascended into the expanse like surface to air missiles. There were four of us now positioned where Heaven meets Earth, levitating to the right and the left of the King of Majesty. It felt like Family. Each one of us had a different color flame, representing our unique gifts and how we affect the Earth, both as individuals and as a team. It reminds me of the Voltron cartoon. Separate, they were powerful, but united, they were unstoppable. As amazing as I felt before, with all four of us, the feeling was even more exhilarating. It was like a power surge as their energy increased my own. My mental capacity unlocked, and I knew all of my thoughts and connected telepathically with their thoughts. Love, honor, and respect for them arose in my heart. I burned with passion for them, and I could feel their love for me. Spirit and truth connected us. Nothing would be impossible for us in this transformation.

When I was in this state, I could fly all around, just like the superheroes. Faith was not even an issue. We knew that God could do anything. It was almost as if we were in "flying fortresses" of fire and power in which fear and doubt had no possibility of penetrating. The all-consuming love of God nullified anything that tried to attack or resist us. The only thing that was able to affect us in this state-of-being came from within. For a brief moment, I felt proud as I floated above the quarry as if I was the one flying out of my own strength. Just as these thoughts crept in, I fell into the water below. It was there for our protection, to keep us safe when we would (not if) fall. I climbed back up the rocks to my place by the prophet, then re-encountered Jesus just as before, and returned to my place by His side in the sky.

This experience opened my eyes to the bigger picture, and I began to realize that there was a lot more going on than I could see. It was a radical, life-changing encounter for my friends and me, but we were simply a link in a long chain that stretched throughout history. It represented the church of the ages moving through God's unfolding plan. There were those who were deceived, those who witnessed the encounters, and those who became the encounters. The antichrist in the false cloud wasn't who most think of from modern theology. It was a deception that crept in when the people positioned themselves for new encounters with Jesus. I saw that this had occurred many times in history and often aborted the authentic revival before it was even born. Likewise, there were those who encountered the true Jesus and shook the Earth in revival and awakening. As for us, this was our moment, we rose to the occasion and became the encounter.

LIGHTING THE DARK

From our place in the sky, we could see the top of the rock quarry—church. Beyond it was a thick blackness. Out from the dark multitudes were streaming over the edge into the church. As all of us became aware of this, our mission downloaded into our hearts, and without hesitation, all of us flew out into the darkness, fanning out into different directions.

The further I went into the darkness, the darker it became. Even though it was pitch black, I could still see. There were people below me going through their daily lives. The light of Christ was shining through me. I watched as His light illuminated them and eliminated the darkness. They began moving towards the direction of the church. I looked back and saw that the path had been lit up by the trail of fire following me. There were now multitudes rushing toward the church. Even from this distance, I could see Jesus above the sky, enthroned in majesty. Once His light pierced their hearts, they went straight into the rock quarry. Amazingly, everyone seemed to make it. No one turned back towards the darkness after beholding His light. A revolution was taking place.

As I looked, I saw flashes of light launching into the sky from the quarry and exploding into fireballs. They were experiencing Jesus just as we had and were being sent out too, lighting the way to Jesus, and sending as many as they could find into the church to become disciples. The new believers would sit in fellowship next to the prophet until they matured into their destiny. Once they could fly, they were sent to fulfill the apostolic commission. There was a pattern of people coming out of the darkness into the light, encountering Jesus, and flying back out into the darkness to send even more people into the light. This cycle went on from generation to generation, ever increasing and ever expanding.

My last glimpse revealed the spreading of the light and the growth of the church. The areas behind me that were once dark were now light and continued to push back the darkness in front of me.

THE **CELESTIAL LANDSCAPE** OF **HEAVEN AND EARTH** WAS **REVIVED** IN THE **LIGHT** AS **KINGDOM FAMILY** TOOK THEIR **RIGHTFUL PLACE** IN THE **HEAVENLIES.**

When I woke up in the morning, I was almost in shock. I didn't know what to do or to think, if I should tell anyone, or even how to act. Was this from God? Yes, I seriously asked that question. The answer didn't come until I was at a FIRE Church service that night, and Dr. Gladstone, the very leader who in the dream represented the prophet, preached a message that confirmed many things in the dream. When I went home after the meeting, it began to settle in my spirit. I have been unpacking it ever since. There are even other more mysterious parts of the dream I have yet to comprehend. It has marked my life as it seems to ever-unfold. Continuous revelation is the essence of a genuine encounter.

THE TIME HAS COME

I am driven every day by this dream. It has become the foundation for my vision and calling, and how I see God and relate to the church. I long to see this fulfilled. Night dreams are given to enable day dreams. I live the impossible in the night dream so I can believe for the impossible in the day dream. I am given over to seeing this dream fulfilled. I want to fly and have faith as I did in the dream. I want to help build, equip, and live life with a church that functions the way God showed me in the dream. He showed me for a reason, and that reason has become the passion and purpose for my life.

It took nearly two decades, two versions of this book, and countless continuous encounters with Jesus just to arrive the description of this dream I was able to share here. This edition of the book is the third season of my life of pointed focus on this dream. Each time there is greater knowledge and revelation. God gave wisdom in seed form, which had to grow before I had any idea of what to do with it. The process of trying to understand it unlocked it for me.

EVERYTHING IN **GOD**, WHETHER **PAST, PRESENT,** OR **FUTURE** IS A **CONSTANTLY EXPANDING ENCOUNTER**.

Encounters are eternally designed. Just as moments with your lover affect you today, so do moments with God affect you for eternity.

The time we are living in now signifies that the next phase of the fulfillment of the dream is at hand. In the many years since this encounter, "Heaven on Earth" has become a language people understand. The church has awakened to the reality of the supernatural. We are on the precipice of the spectacular. Awareness of the impossible becoming attainable is transforming belief systems. Once the barriers are ripped away, limitless ideas begin to burn in the hearts of the children of God.

THE **BODY** OF **CHRIST** IS READY TO **TAKE** HER **PLACE** IN THE **SKY** AND **SHINE** THE **LIGHT** OF **JESUS** TO **ALL CREATION**.

ACTIVATION

God desires us to desire encounters with Him. In the Sky Dream, I was in fellowship with brothers in the Lord and in relationship with leaders in the church, which empowered me to recognize the authentic encounter with Jesus. We should not be afraid of the supernatural. This is who we are created to be. If you surround yourself with leaders who can guide you and speak into your life, you are in a safe place to experience more of God.

The main thing in the dream that kept me aware when the deceiving cloud appeared was my own relationship with Jesus. What happened on the outside did not harmonize with the Jesus relationship I had on the inside. Keep Jesus the center of your life's gaze, and you will hit the target every time.

The encounter I had in the dream reminds me of two encounters in the Bible that I love to visualize. The first one, found in Daniel 7:9-10 and 13-14, is the encounter with the Ancient of Days. The context of the whole passage is similar to the dream because the appearance of the fiery throne drives out the deceiver. The next passage is Ezekiel 1:4-28. I feel that it is the most descriptive encounter of the glory of God in Scripture. It reminds me of the brightness of my encounter with the way it reveals Jesus. Although my dream was not identical to these encounters, there is a Scriptural precedent for what I experienced. As I stated in chapter one, the Bible is a guide for us to experience our own encounters with God.

Take a few moments to read through both of these Biblical encounters. Ask God to take you there, and allow you to see what both Daniel and Ezekiel saw. Ask Him to allow you to experience what they experienced. Write out the encounter below.

Daniel's Encounter:

Ezekiel's Encounter:

A lifestyle of encounters fuels our existence. If this encounter inspired you to pursue your own encounters with Jesus, then take a few moments here to ask Him for it. This will be a visualization activation. Turn on the eyes of your imagination—the eyes of your spirit. Pray through each step, and ask God to open up that reality for you. Afterward, write out what you experienced.

1. Visualize yourself in the rock quarry, and Jesus appears before you in the sky. What do you see?

2. Visualize yourself flying into the sky to meet Him. What do you experience?

3. Visualize yourself flying into the Earth, bringing the light of Christ with you. What is happening?

DECLARATION

I declare that I will encounter Jesus. I declare that I will become the encounter. I declare that I will bring light to the darkness of the world. I declare that Heaven will touch the Earth through my life!

RISE REVIVALISTS!

THREE

GOD DARES US TO DREAM

DREAMERS BELIEVE FOR THE **IMPOSSIBLE.**

They are stargazers, wonderers, and adventurers. They are not satisfied with "normal" life. They desire to live the life of an extraordinaire. Those who choose to remain in the norm—the monotonous continuum that life "throws at you"—will never realize their full potential. "Normal" people don't change the world. "Normal" people who decide to break out of the mundane, do!

As believers, this is a culture in which we must stand out and not stand in. We are the ones who demonstrate to society that there is more than the "every day," more than the "normal." We must look to the future; we must become dreamers. Even if your life seems normal—if you are eternity conscious—then you are different, viewing life from a paradigm that many forfeit due to the lack of bravery needed to "go against the grain." If you live from eternity, your life will stamp the times with meaning and significance for generations to come. You contain, in your relationship with Jesus, the substance the Earth is searching for. And that something inside of you is the culture that will influence the world. Realizing who you are and what you have access to in your relationship with Jesus empowers you to change the world. You become something different, something other, something heavenly.

Our dreams, whether a day dream, a night dream, or a life aspiration, are catalysts that drive us forward. They unlock our inner desires and make a path for them to come true. My Sky Dream perpetually enhances the vision I have for my life. I experienced things in the dream that are impossible here on the Earth. God showed me in the dream that the impossible is possible, and that things I experienced there, I can also experience here.

THE **REASON** OUR **DREAMS** ARE SO **POWERFUL** IS BECAUSE OUR **SUBCONSCIOUS** IS **FREE TO BELIEVE** WHAT OUR **MINDS WILL NOT.**

In dream-state, there are no limitations. If we can dream while we are awake, then the same wonders we encounter while sleeping will begin to flow into our lives. We will find ourselves doing the impossible and living in a state of unbreakable faith. Such a lifestyle will reflect the life of Jesus in our modern generation. The world around us will see those who carry Heaven to Earth.

DREAMS OPEN UP THE **WORLD** OF **IMPOSSIBILITIES** AND BRING THE **FUTURE** INTO THE **PRESENT.**

Dreamers are the architects of tomorrow. So, believe it, dream it, and go for it.

JACOB'S DREAM

The Bible is full of dreamers. None of which is probably more recognizable than Jacob. Jacob's dream was a turning point in his life and became part of the history of the nation of Israel. He dreamed of Heaven meeting Earth. Without even comprehending it, Jacob found himself at a connecting point between the natural world and the supernatural world.

> And he dreamed, and behold, there was a ladder set up on the earth, and the top of it reached to heaven. And behold the angels of God were ascending and descending on it! And behold, the LORD stood above it and said, "I am the LORD, the God of Abraham your father and the God of Isaac. The land on which you lie I will give to you and to your offspring.
>
> Genesis 28:12-13 ESV

This wasn't meant to be just a cool story we can read our kids about a ladder that reaches to heaven. This was monumental. This dream was a prophecy of Jesus, which continues to impact the Earth with the reality of Heaven. I say, "Lord, fulfill your words in acts and let us dream these kinds of dreams once again, O God."

Generations before this, mankind tried to build in his own strength a "Stairway to Heaven." At the Tower of Babel, we witness man's attempt to find its way to the Creator. They were reaching for the sky with all the muster of their natural ability and power (Genesis 11). Who knows how far the human race could have advanced in technology by that time? What if it was not as archaic as we have always imagined? What if their tower was the most technologically advanced building the world has ever seen? If so, they were using it with the intention of finding their place in the sky.

I ask these questions to bring the story into the modern timeframe. When we think of it this way, we capture the essence of the story with more understanding. This visualization creates a reenactment in our minds, causing us to realize just how massively significant their attempt was.

Humans building a way to God with their "own hands" is the crescendo of the religious spirit. Human advancement is at its pinnacle when it reveals the glory of God. However, they used it to try to build sky-bridge to God, guiding themselves instead of being guided by God.

The collective human race assembled in a singular project. Unity like this is "unheard of." The audacity of building a city with a tower that rose into the heavens was a marvelous endeavor. Such unity, however, originated in the spirit of man, not the spirit of God. They were building outside of His image. The city itself became the greatest idol the world had ever seen. It was an attempt to forge a connection to God without using His plans—later to be revealed as Jesus.

God, in mercy, intervened and confused them, stopping the construction of the tower. They were united without Him, not through Him, which is why they were scattered. The city and the tower reflected what they could do, not what God was doing through them. God spread them across the Earth to save them from their own methods and reset in their relation to each other. Their achievement soared, but it wasn't Heaven on Earth. It wasn't born of God. It didn't bear His image. "Give to Caesar what is Caesar, give to God what is God's," (Mark 12:17).

THE TRUE CONNECTION TO HEAVEN

God desires us to untie with Him in the heavenlies (Eph 2:6). He gives Jacob the dream as a blueprint for the secret of Heaven on Earth, which is the cry of the human heart—intimacy with God. Jacob was the first to glimpse into this reality. Therefore, God built a nation around the one who dreamed of Heaven on Earth and named it Israel.

> Your offspring shall be like the dust of the earth, and you shall spread abroad to the west and to the east and to the north and to the south, and in you and your offspring shall all the families of the earth be blessed. Behold, I am with you and will keep you wherever you go, and will bring you back to this
>
> land. For I will not leave you until I have done what I have promised you.
>
> vv 14-15 ESV

We have the perspective to look back through history and see how the impact of this dream fanned out and influenced the world. It is both timeless and generational. It was not just a dream about land, but about land filled with people who walk in the presence of God.

THE **DREAM** IS A **CALL** FOR A **LAND** TO BE **INHABITED** BY **THOSE** WHO **ABIDE** IN **HEAVEN**.

It is an introduction to the vision that took hold of Jacob's heart. This nation then became the only nation in the world that had the true connection to God. Through such a nation, God chose to fulfill the dream and send the Ladder that would connect Heaven and Earth. Only through them could he send his Son. This nation became the cocoon through which the entire world would once again be filled with the knowledge of God, calling all nations into fellowship with the Son. After the reset at the Tower of Babel, God chose a nation through which the Master Architect would come and show the collective human race the true way for Heaven to inhabit the Earth. He, Himself was and is the connection.

> Truly, truly I say to you, you will see the heavens opened and the angels of God ascending and descending on the Son of Man.
>
> John 1:51 NASB

All of Israel not only knew of Jacob's dream but built their existence on it. And here is Jesus fulfilling it on the Earth in plain sight. As he shared this prophecy, those present would've made an immediate correlation to Jacob's dream.

Jesus saw Nathanael coming to Him, and said of him, "Behold, an Israelite indeed, in whom there is no deceit!" Nathanael said to Him, "How do You know me?" Jesus answered and said to him, "Before Philip called you, when you were under the fig tree, I saw you." Nathanael answered Him, "Rabbi, You are the Son of God; You are the King of Israel." Jesus answered and said to him, "Because I said to you that I saw you under the fig tree, do you believe? You will see greater things than these.

John 1:48-50 ESV

The secret is that when we believe, it establishes a connection. Here, Jesus is explaining to Nathanael that he too will see in the same spiritual dimension in which Jesus saw him under the fig tree. The ones who see are able to open the eyes of those who do not. As we learn to navigate the supernatural realm, we will gain the ability to unlock the gift in others and activate them in their heavenly residency.

WHERE HEAVEN MEETS EARTH

The House of God is anywhere Heaven meets Earth. A true church will be a fellowship of union—a church who knows Jesus cannot live divided from her heavenly identity. God resides where there is a connection, where there are those who are plugged-in. While writing this, I drove around looking for a wifi connection. I needed a place to connect. In the same way, the Earth needs those who are connected to Heaven. Anywhere this happens, God's house is being built and established.

WE ARE HEAVEN'S WIFI SIGNAL, NETWORK, AND SYSTEM. WE RECEIVE, BECOME, AND TRANSMIT HEAVEN ON EARTH.

> For just as lightning comes from the west and flashes
> even to the west, so will the coming of the Son of Man be.
> Matthew 24:27 NASB

Jesus announced that His return would be like lightning, which was not an accident. It is the ultimatum of Heaven and Earth colliding. Our lives should prophesy the fulfillment of this. We are living epistles, enacting what is going to happen. John G. Lake described the power of God on him as "lightnings" in his hands. Even though we live on the Earth, our homes are in heavenly places.

WE ARE BI-UNIVERSAL

There is a parallel universe—the supernatural realm. Not only do we have access there, but we also have authority there because we are seated next to the One who owns all authority. The role of the church is to administer Heaven on Earth.

We are called to a higher existence. We are called to live like we were created—in the image of God. There is a chasm of sin—a way of life lived outside of the image of God—separating men from God that is completely destroyed by faith in Jesus.

Jacob's dream gives insight into the meaning of life. His dream opens the door to endless possibilities. God showed Jacob how He builds his house on the Earth. He uses people connected to Heaven. This house constitutes apostolic and prophetic fulfillment. Creation connected to Creator—kids connected to their Father—is the revival of His household.

Separation was never part of the plan. We were never meant to live outside of Father's house. His presence should not be a foreign substance. Yes, His presence encompasses the Earth, but most of humanity is unaware. We are supposed to abide, to thrive, to function, in this place. This is a place man can once again find God. God's house is where supernatural activity takes place. The world is going to be full of these houses. If it's not connected to Heaven, then it's not in the network. Our calling is to be those who are connected and help others to get connected and stay connected. This network covers the whole world.

GOD WANTS EVERYONE EVERYWHERE TO EXPERIENCE HIM.

Revelation is the foundation of the house that God is building today, which is the church. The church does not replace Israel's call. It helps to fulfill it. Jesus said, "on this rock"—revelation that He is the Son of God, the Ladder, the Connection of Heaven to Earth—"I will build my church, and the gates of hell shall not prevail against it," (see Matthew 16:18). There is an unfolding plan of God between Jacob's dream and the ladder being a foundation for Israel, and Jesus being the ladder, which is the foundation of the church He is building today.

Only the culture of Heaven can change the culture of the world. This culture comes from Heaven through the church. The church is the Ecclesia and Koinonia: A fellowship that governs the gateway of Heaven in the Earth. We reveal what Heaven is like through our church Family, awakening fulfillment in the hearts of creation and setting them free from bondage to temporal existence.

Bethel Church in Redding California, led by Pastor Bill Johnson, is a prime example of a place where God is building His house. Bill's book, *When Heaven Invades Earth,* has transformed the lives of many. It describes what it is actually like to live in a church Family and culture that is heavenly. Bethel's heart is to see His Kingdom come on Earth as it is in Heaven. Bethel is God's house, and God's house is where Heaven meets the Earth. They have fulfilled their namesake and amazing fashion and given all of us a heavenly vision and mandate.

It is clear that we do not have to wait until eternity to partake of these heavenly things, but that we have access to them now. The culmination of it is the return of the King. Until then we prepare the way through generating "where Heaven meets Earth" experiences everywhere we go. Every time we do this, we prophesy the reality that Jesus is coming again. Preaching is simply anything we say or do that reveals Heaven on Earth. When we abide in His house, Heaven abides in us in the Earth. Without saying or doing anything, we resonate His presence. Heaven is revealed in our speech, actions, and being. It is who we are.

WHO WE ARE

We exist where worlds collide. We inhabit the dwellings of angels. We function in the midst of the celestial. We are born of the Spirit. The spiritual realm is our domain. Our address is registered in Heaven. We have the keys to unlock the "Sands of Time." Our destiny is the demonstration of the power of God. Our call is Heaven coming to Earth. Does this sound metaphorical? Does this sound like a dream? I could continue. Are you captivated, intrigued, or angered by these statements?

I cannot even capture the essence of them derived from the Word, much less the amplitude of their fulfillment.

Some reserve things like this for the millennium because they've been taught a theology that the supernatural is only past and future, but not present. However, we have access to all the power of Heaven here and now. Imagine such a walk, as my friend Scott Thompson once explained, that when you die, "you don't go anywhere," because you're already in Heaven. Does that sound crazy? Is there a Scriptural precedent to even ask such a question? Do you think that Enoch and Elijah may have figured something out? They did not die; they just transitioned from one reality to another. They achieved such revelation of Heaven on the inside that it swallowed them up on the outside. Internally, they were filled with Heaven to the degree that the fulfillment of what was happening to them became a physical entrance into Heaven. They entered through the gate of life, not the gate of death. And the relationship they had with God was in the Old Covenant. How much more in the New? They "bent the theory" and pulled the future into the present of their lives, and experienced the magnitude of God's power. Were the special? Was it just for them, or were they prototypes of something that is available for all of us?

What I am trying to do is open our eyes to more. MORE! Even as Christians there is something inside us that cries out for more. We are created in His image, and He is supernatural. Jesus Himself is the embodiment of both the elements of Heaven and the elements of Earth. In this life, we can experience as much of Heaven as we have the faith for.

WE CAN **CAPTIVATE** A **GENERATION** WITH THE **LOVE** OF **GOD.**

I am dreaming out loud here. Can you dream with me? Can we look together through the keyhole in the door and dare to believe for the impossible, the astonishing, the things for which there are no words—no explanation, but our hearts seem to burn for? Who are we? We are the impossible ones!

HERE COMES THIS DREAMER

Jacob's dream was the foundation for all that his son Joseph would accomplish. Joseph's dream was a continuation and fulfillment of Jacob's. Joseph dreamed that his brothers were bowing down to him (Genesis 37:1-11), which was a necessary component of God making a way to bring the people back to His land after the coming famine. Joseph had several dreams about this and would relay it to his father, who was also a dreamer. Jacob loved Joseph because he was the son of "his old age" (3), but I also think that he loved him more because he too was a dreamer. However, his brothers despised him because of it. They were not dreamers like their father and brother. They could not understand the significance of Joseph's dream and how it related to fulfilling their father's dream. "They said to one another, 'Here comes this dreamer!'" Compared to his brothers, Joseph was abnormal. He had a dream and saw something from above changing the realities here on the Earth.

Those who dare to dream are often unsettling to those who do not. This was the case with Joseph's brothers. Their lack of connection with heavenly realities caused them to be jealous when it should've inspired them into their own encounters. This dream was also vital to his brothers fulfilling their own callings as well. Instead of embracing the dream, they misunderstood their roles in it. The position you are presently in may be the gateway—the Bethel experience—that takes you into a season of breakthrough. In the end, the place of serving their younger brother was actually a massive upgrade in their lifestyle. It looked like a step back for them, when in reality it was a step up.

The dreamers are the ones with the instinct to see the "door in the floor" that leads to greatness. The ability to recognize and celebrate the promotion of others is vital in realizing our promotions and fulfilling our dreams. Celebrating their dreams will launch us into our own.

DREAM GOD'S DREAM

Let us dream as Jacob, Joseph, and so many others that went before us who found something heavenly. Let us dream God's dream with Him. The one thing that can truly unite the world is not the understanding of religion, but the love of Christ. When we have this, we can see people as Jesus sees them and our hate-filled hearts will be filled with love.

THE SAD CONSEQUENCE OF HELL IS THAT IT IS NOT THE ABSENCE OF GOD'S LOVE, BUT THE REJECTION OF HIS LOVE THAT SENDS ONE THERE.

The world's desperate cry will be answered by us when we dream. Dreams create vision. Vision creates calling. Calling creates action. Action creates disciples. Disciples don't merely change society? Rather, they recreate the culture of Heaven here on the Earth!

Imagine a company of dreamers who dream the things of God. "God dares us to dream" is a phrase Holy Spirit dropped in my heart one day as I was meditating on how we are seated in heavenly places. I was dreaming beyond what I was experiencing, and it gave me the vision to get there. To dream beyond our experience keeps our lives in the current flowing from Heaven.

> Where there is no prophetic vision the people cast off restraint, but blessed is he who keeps the law.
>
> Proverbs 29:18 ESV

God wants us to day dream, to night dream, and to imagine all the things we can become when we dream of Him. God dares us to dream. Jacob, the dreamer, fathered Joseph, who was a dream prodigy. At a young age, he began to make an impact with his Godly gifts. If we dream, we can make the same impact. Become a dreamer... Dream again... Dream anew...

ACTIVATION

Night Dream: You can unlock and activate dreams in your own life. Ask God for a dream tonight. Keep a journal or a recorder close by so you can retain the details of the dream. If you don't understand it, pray into it, share it with friends, or search for resources on dream interpretation, such as materials by John Paul Jackson. In my book, *Activating a Prophetic Lifestyle*, I share how to interpret and apply prophetic revelations. I recommend it for dreams as well.

Life Dream: Write down dreams yet to be fulfilled in your life, and ask God for strategies to see them realized.

DECLARATION

I will dream dreams with God. I will pursue the impossible and establish my life as a Bethel, a house of God in the Earth. I will be a hot spot—one who connects Heaven to Earth, a lightning bolt who flashes with the power of God in my generation.

RISE REVIVALISTS!

FOUR

PROPHETIC PRODIGIES

IMAGINE A **SCHOOL** THAT **EQUIPS YOU** TO BECOME A **SUPERHERO.**

"The 'Superhero Training Academy' is now taking applications for the Fall semester." Would you be interested? What if they could teach you how to fly, walk on water, translocate, or telepathy? What if all the powers you read about in the comics were available to you, and all you had to do was attend this school? I'd be the first in line.

I am a graduate of FIRE School of Ministry, which was born in the midst of the Brownsville Revival in Pensacola, FL, where I also attended their ministry school (BRSM). In addition, I taught for several years at Bethel Atlanta School of Supernatural Ministry (BASSM), which is a school plant from the fires of revival burning at Bethel Church in Redding, CA. I am very familiar with and passionate about schools like this. I have also been a guest teacher at similar ministry schools. From my time as a student at FIRE to my time as a teacher at BASSM, there has been an amazing expansion and growth in activating a supernatural lifestyle and equipping the children of God in the miraculous power of God. I believe one of the expressions of authenticity is for the church to equip in this manner. Likewise, much of my vision for what I believe God has designed for me to do in life filters through my experience in these schools.

Both as a student and as a teacher, I have grown tremendously in my own spiritual gifts and activated hundreds of students to discover their amazing gifts as well. Nevertheless, I have yet to see a school like the one I imagined above. My wife and I have always dreamt of it and believed that it was possible, but I have yet to witness someone demonstrate it in our generation. Who knows, by the time you read this, we may have started one.

In the Sky Dream, my friends and I were flying all over the Earth performing signs and wonders, just like we read about the Apostles did in the book of Acts. We do live in a fantastic time, and I have heard about stories both presently, and in church history where this is beginning to take place, but it's only in pockets—happening here or there. I have seen glimmers, but nothing full scale.

After a conversation with a friend one day, I became aware of the fact that I could dream a whole lot bigger. We were dialoguing about such things when he made the astonishing declaration, "I want to start a prophetic school that would be similar to Xavier's School for Gifted Youngsters," referencing the Superhero Comic Series, *The X Men.* In the series, Charles Xavier, also known as Professor X, heads up a school for young ones who have mutant or supernatural powers. He brings them into this school to train them how to use and control their special gifts. These are full-blown superheroes you'd watch on TV doing the absolute impossible... And learning to get better at it!

The goal of a prophetic school would be to find those with prophetic and supernatural gifts of the Spirit and raise them up and equip them in an environment that doesn't quench their gifts, but shows them how to use them. What if, for illustration's sake, we replace Professor X with Jesus and the gifted youngsters with the disciples?" The School of Disciples Jesus lead was both a prototype and an archetype school. He demonstrated all the gifts, not to show or prove he was God, but to show earthly men how to be heavenly.

JESUS TAUGHT THE **DISCIPLES** HOW TO **HEAR FATHER'S VOICE, TURN WATER** INTO **WINE, WALK** ON **WATER, HEAL** THE **SICK, RAISE** THE **DEAD, CAST** OUT **DEMONS,** AND **TRANSFIGURE** THEIR **BODIES**.

The environment of His classroom was a daily supernatural lab, with all the wonders and gifts of the Spirit in full operation. The graduates of this school—the Apostles and the community surrounding them—went on to reproduce the "acts" of Jesus to their generation. Some of the stories in Acts are more incredible than the comics.

It is easy to become so accustomed to the stories many of us grew up hearing that we miss the supernatural factor that bathed everything Jesus said and did. His "school" was the foundation of the church. They were known for being supernatural. They were known for being like Jesus. The Book of Acts is what it looked like when His students graduated.

Nowadays, in many circles of Christendom, if you are known for being like Jesus, or doing the same miracles that he did, then they label you as a heretic or under the influence of a demon. This opinion is Pharisaical thinking. Such a mindset is the exact opposite of the reality that Jesus demonstrated for us.

JESUS SHOWED US WHAT IT IS LIKE FOR MEN AND WOMEN TO WALK IN THE FULLNESS OF HEAVEN.

He was and is the ultimate Teacher. It's not just in what He said or did; it's also in how He did it. Everything was of His Father's design. Imagine a school where this model was the foundation for how they did everything.

When I glean from comics, it gives me an attachment point to consider just how fulfilling a supernatural lifestyle could be. I am not making the statement that the entirety of the *X-Men* series is Godly, but we can capture the heart of the writer's desire to know the supernatural. God created everyone in His image. Therefore, His image can shine through someone's creativity, even if they don't realize it. However, it does give us a beautiful picture for a school of this caliber.

SCHOOL OF THE YOUNG PROPHETS

I feel these are just the very beginning stages for what is to come in training people in the supernatural. When I graduated FIRE in 2001, there were only a few schools like this in America. In 2006, Dr. Gladstone prophesied a "School of the Young Prophets" soon to emerge. The prophecy was from a dream in which he encountered a group of young people who personified the majesty of God. He knew the time was coming when young prophets like these would arise. New ministry schools launched in the years to follow. Supernatural training centers are now all over the globe. I believe this first wave of schools is serving as a prototype for future generations. More schools will arise and become precise examples of training the saints just as Jesus taught the disciples. I believe the church itself will shift into a disciple-making model as if the schools and the church morph into the image of the church I saw in my Sky Dream. For Jesus and his disciples, the school was the church.

In the current church culture, it would be unusual to find a structure in place designed to raise up young men and women with supernatural and prophetic abilities. A wineskin of creativity is the key to seeing a church emerge with a culture that celebrates the gifts of the body without misunderstanding them. In contrast, the world seeks out gifted youngsters and promotes them into their genius.

A prodigy is a young person who demonstrates abilities that have advanced beyond their years. Special schools exist to train up prodigies in their specific skills. There are schools of music, including, classical, jazz, contemporary, rock, etc. There are also schools of art, categorized into training for specific mediums. There are also schools for all the other skills prodigies may exhibit designed to ensure they get the best education available to maximize their potential.

What would the comparison be for the supernatural if it existed? Could you imagine a school for the apostolic, prophetic, and evangelistic, with sections on healing, miracles, prophecy, and speaking in tongues? What an amazing dream! How many supernatural prodigies have gone unrecognized by the church? How many bypassed their admittance to the

School of the Young Prophets? Lord, grant us eyes to identify and champion prophetic prodigies in our midst.

PRODIGY

A *prodigy* is "a person, esp. a child, possessing unusual or marvelous talents; anything that causes wonder or amazement; something monstrous or abnormal." Prodigy is also an archaic word for *Omen*. An omen is "a phenomenon or prophetic significance." Prodigy in Latin origin basically means "speaking monster." We usually develop negative thoughts with the word *monster*, but it essentially means "something of unnatural size, shape, or quality; being an enormity or a marvel." It seems it referred to something extraordinary that over the years was most often attributed to the things that were evil because of a negative worldview that began to influence the church, diluting supernatural experience.

Prodigies are extraordinary ones. Based on these definitions, we could label a prodigy as a person who is an omen to their generation. In other words, the prodigy is the gifted person with such prophetic significance that they are the sign and wonder the world is looking for.

We will take a closer look at David shortly, but here is a teenager that killed a giant. Before that, he was even killing lions and bears. There was more to David, as Samuel found out, than "meets the eye." He may have looked normal on the outside, but he was abnormal on the inside. He had a secret life with God that was unknown to everyone except God. When the pressure came, he was revealed to the world as a prodigy. God saw that and sent Samuel to anoint him in his calling as king, even at a young age (1 Samuel 16).

I feel like there are young David's all around us. They already have awesome histories with God. They need fathers and mothers to nurture them. Prodigies have giftings, but need the guidance of wisdom to mature into their destines.

IT IS THE **JOY** OF **TRUE FATHERS** AND **MOTHERS** TO **SEE** THEIR **SONS** AND **DAUGHTERS OUTSHINE THEM.**

Their desire is for their kids to take the baton of the Lord from their generation and carry further than ever before.

THE CALL DC AND AZUSA NOW

The Call DC was an event held Washington, DC in 2000. It was a gathering of 400,000 people on the National Mall, organized by the revivalist, Lou Engle. The goal was to call the young people to gather together to fast and pray for the nation to turn their heart's back to God. Well-known speakers went to give a charge for reformation.

BRSM chartered 18 buses for the students to make the epic drive from Pensacola to DC. I was super excited about the trip. Heroes of mine would be there sharing their hearts.

Twenty-four hours later, we arrived. We fasted the whole trip, so we were already famished by the time the event began. We were right up front near the stage, soaking in all that the Lord had for us. However, as the day wore on, we became more and more drained, which made it tough to stay engaged. Still, it was a momentous experience in my life. Since then, The Call has held events all over, and I count it as an honor to have been at the first one.

Out of all the glorious experiences from that day, the most impactful moment for me was when Lou Engle's [then] 13-year-old son, Jesse, prayed for the assembly. His prayer was simple, direct, and profound:

"LORD, RAISE THEM UP AT 12, INSTEAD OF 21!"

As a 20-year-old, his statement stunned me. Here was a young man praying like few I had ever heard in front of thousands with strength, courage, and power. He was larger than life, surpassing the stereotype of a typical boy his age. I thought to myself, "I wish I had heard that at 12 rather than 20." Kids and teenagers must not lose their childhood, but even in their youth, they can become signs and wonders in their generation.

Fourteen years later at a Jesus Culture conference in Atlanta, I had the pleasure to meet Lou Engle and tell him the story of how his son impacted me. I also shared that I wrote about it in this book and even sent him a copy of the first edition. Encouraged by my story, he talked about how The Call was transitioning from a "John the Baptist Movement" to a "New Jesus Movement."

Fast-forward two years, I found myself working on the second edition of this book as I sat at Bethel Atlanta watching the live-stream of Azusa Now—another event organized by The Call and Lou Engle. It was held at the Rose Bowl in Los Angeles on April 9th, 2016, to commemorate the 110th anniversary of the Azusa Street Revival. Over 70,000 attended and a million-plus watched live. It's surreal that as I wrote, watching the meeting unfold, what was happening, related directly to this book and the stories it contains. It was like I was a reporter capturing a moment of heavenly history. I was considering how both events affected my life, the church, and the future when the Lord showed me a picture of how it all ties together:

> Azusa Now is completing a 16-year circuit that began at the Call DC. Many of the things that we prayed for when I was there have now become a reality. And, what we pray for today will not take another 16 years; its response will be immediate. It's like the second rocket booster, ready to complete the transition of Heaven to Earth. The two events complete the arc of the rainbow, positioning us for the pot of gold.

Right after I received this word, Jesse emerged on the stage and began to share about The Call DC and how it related to Azusa Now. WOW! Coincidences that seem random and unrelated are often a glimpse into the blueprints of Heaven. As I'm typing out how all of this ties together, he starts sharing, 2000 miles away, the same things. If you are reading this, then you are privileged to capture in a few sentences what it took those of us who lived out the 16-year cycle to see how it all tied together. The beauty of it is that our experience invites you to inherit the legacy of the journey.

SAGA

What is a "prophetic prodigy?" Peculiarly enough, I stumbled across this statement while prophesying to a young lady I will call Saga. She was 15-years-old at the time, and the amount of the depth of God I saw in her was mind-blowing. Even to look into her eyes was a prophetic experience. It was like seeing the things past being fulfilled by the things to come, right in front of me. You knew that Jesus lived in her because

His personality and gifts were shining through her. "She's a prophetic prodigy," Holy Spirit whispered to me.

I finally saw what Jesse Engle was praying for in the eyes a 15-year-old girl. Once I heard the prophecy contained within the prayer, I was in search of its fulfillment. When I stood face-to-face with Heaven shining in purity through her as the embodiment of the prophecy, I realized the enormity of it was more significant than I imagined. It was better than I dreamed it would be. She was alive in God, and God was alive in her.

Our young people are supposed to be empowered. Imagine what David, at the age of 17, felt after Samuel poured all that oil on his head as a young man. Purpose, faith, excitement, and calling flooded his soul. He had something to live for, and more than that, it was something from God. His call was not limited to his life or his generation; it was a call for the ages. His life from that point on was being driven by that prophetic word. How he reacted to the world around him flowed through the prism of the prophecy. He grew up knowing God saw him as a King. He had an eternal destiny stamped on his DNA.

I got saved when I was 16-years-old. I can only imagine what it would've been like to receive a prophetic word like that at that age. I would have given my life to it, to fulfill it, to learn about it, and to become it.

PROPHETIC POTENTIAL

Akiane Kramarik, now in her twenties, was a child binary genius. At eight-years-old, she painted a masterpiece called Prince of Peace, which is a larger-than-life-size painting of a vision she had of Jesus. The story of God speaking to her as a little child was told on TV shows and in movies. Her parents didn't understand what was happening to her at first, but they went with it and allowed her to cultivate her gifts. As she grew up, her paintings transformed lives all over the world. She is an example of a prophetic prodigy, nurtured in a home that appreciated her supernatural abilities.

Akiane and Saga have opened up a whole new understanding to me of operating in the things of God at young ages. I believe this may be part of the reason why Jesus guarded the little children and had them come unto Him (Matthew 19:14). He knew the prophetic potential that brewed within them and was jealous to preserve it. Even some of the disciples were still teenagers when Jesus called them.

Age is not the centrality of the matter. To become a prophetic prodigy is to find God in a new way, and access what He has already deposited inside you. David was already king, Samuel simply activated David's true identity. My goal is that as you read this, you will also be activated, and realize your true identity in Christ.

Each new day we are closer to the day when Jesus will return to the Earth, and we have the opportunity to see a part of Him we have never seen before. If you can capture that, it is like reading fine music. Without ever hearing it, the sound of the symphony echoes through the corridors of your mind and spirit, as you mentally tie the notes together in an internal harmony. You experience what you cannot see through the power of imagination.

IMAGINATION DEVELOPS **FAITH** FOR THE
IMPOSSIBLE TO BECOME **ATTAINABLE.**

There is a new breed of prophetic prodigies in the earth. They have "eyes to see" that which generations-past have overlooked. They will be pioneers, settlers, and builders for the Kingdom, both in new geographical regions and in new heavenly realities.

> WHEN WE **UNBOX** THE **PROPHETIC**, WE WILL **SEE** IN
> **NEW WAYS** AND **ASCEND** TO **NEW LEVELS**.

The gifts of the Spirit are available to all of us to use at our disposal. We can both become prodigies and raise up prodigies. The spirit of a prodigy within Samuel recognized the spirit of a prodigy within David. Seeing this way will make it an honor to be in the presence of others because you will see them as God sees them. The next prodigy could be in our midst at any moment Likewise, the next prophet to anoint us as prodigies could be coming our way. Let us focus our gaze on our prophetic destinies and the destinies of all whom we encounter.

ACTIVATION

I think the simplest way to summarize a prophetic prodigy would be to say that they are ones who believe their dreams can come true. Therefore, they start experiencing them before society believes it is possible.

What dreams are you expecting to happen quickly in your life?

Inside of David was a king. Who is the prodigy in you?

DECLARATION

Lord, release the prodigy in me. Give me sight to see the prodigy in others. Send someone capable of equipping me with my prophetic destiny and raise me up to equip someone else in their destiny. Release the prophetic prodigies on the Earth. Open up schools for gifted youngsters, oldsters, and everyone in-between.

RISE REVIVALISTS!

FIVE

WHERE ARE THE ELIJAHS?

BY SEEING THE ENCOUNTER, WE BECOME THE ENCOUNTER.

You feel it in your bones. Today is the day. This morning is different. Expectancy is in the air...

You led your nation in one of the most radical encounters the world has ever seen. You fathered a company of prophets and taught them the elements of encounter. A spiritual son is waiting in the wings to carry on your ministry of encounter to the next generation. Today is the day, the culmination, the grand encounter, the one all the others are pointing toward...

Today you will enter into an encounter that will never end...

When you read the Bible, do you ever put yourself "in their shoes"? You may have recognized that I input you into Elijah's story above. What would it have been like to be him on the day that he ascended into Heaven? The Bible comes alive when we visualize ourselves in the stories and realize that the reason the story is present in Scripture is to activate us in our own encounters.

WHERE IS THE LORD, THE GOD OF ELIJAH?

Not too long ago, the question "Where is the Lord, the God of Elijah?" was floating around in many church circles. People were hungry for the supernatural. They were hungry to experience God the way the Bible illustrates. They simply wanted "more."

One of the prime examples of a supernatural lifestyle is the life of Elijah the Prophet. The question asked was the same one Elijah's successor, Elisha, asked just after Elijah flew into heaven via a whirlwind. As Elijah ascended, his mantle fell behind, which represents the anointing—the power of the Holy Spirit in his life. Elisha took hold of the mantle and rolled it up. He approached the Jordan River and cried out, "where is the Lord, the God of Elijah?"

> As they were going along and talking, behold, there appeared a chariot of fire and horses of fire which separated the two of them. And Elijah went up by a whirlwind to heaven. Elisha saw it and cried out, "My father, my father, the chariots of Israel and its horsemen!" And he saw him no more. Then he took hold of his own clothes and tore them in two pieces.

He also took up the mantle of Elijah which fell from him
and returned and stood by the bank of the Jordan.

2 Kings 2:11-13 NASB

At one point, it was as if the half the church was crying out, "Where is the Lord, the God of Elijah?" just as Elisha had that day. "Where is the One I've read about in the Bible, the One who heals the sick and raises the dead, the One who anointed Elijah to ascend into Heaven? Where is the God who does things such as this?" I believe we find the answer to the question contained in the story itself. To start out, Elisha wasn't just "shooting in the dark." Rather, he was demonstrating who God was and who he was through a declaration. He was fulfilling the precedent set moments before by his mentor.

Before Elijah's ascension, he and Elisha had an encounter at the river. As they were walking, Elijah rolled up his mantle and struck the waters, and they parted forming a dry path for them to walk.

> Now fifty men of the sons of the prophets went and stood
> opposite them at a distance, while the two of them stood
> by the Jordan. Elijah took his mantle and folded it
> together and struck the waters, and they were divided
> here and there, so that the two of them crossed over on
> dry ground.

vv 7-8

Elisha was revealing that the same God who parted the waters for Elijah would now part the waters for him. Just as the company of prophets had witnessed Elijah perform this wonder, now they would likewise watch Elisha follow in his footsteps.

He took the mantle of Elijah that fell from him and struck the waters and said "Where is the Lord, the God of Elijah?" And when he also had struck the waters, they were divided here and there; and Elisha crossed over. Now when the sons of the prophets who were at Jericho opposite him saw him, they said, "The spirit of Elijah rests on Elisha." And they came to meet him and bowed themselves to the ground before him.

v 15

Demonstration follows the declaration, revealing to the prophets that the spirit of Elijah was now at rest in Elisha. The same spirit present with Moses and Joshua, highlighting the significance of Elisha's call and authority. They came and bowed in honor and recognition that Elisha was now the prophet of Israel. Elisha's position of honor is met with the same ministry of power Elijah possessed. The power demonstration verifies that Elisha received Elijah's mantle. When the sons of the prophets recognized this, they came and honored Elisha just as they had Elijah.

Let's ponder what this meant. If Elijah were alive today, what would it be like? He could call both fire and rain down from Heaven.

HE **RAISED** THE **DEAD** AND USED **TORNADOS** AS **TAXICABS!**

He was a household name in Israel. At times he stood before the king, which would be like standing before the President today. He revealed God at national assemblies, which would be like having a nationally televised revival on the Washington Mall. He turned his entire nation back to God.

ELIJAH WAS UTTERLY **POSSESSED** BY THE **SPIRIT** OF **GOD**; SO MUCH SO THAT **HE** WOULD NOT EVEN **FACE DEATH**, BUT BE **TAKEN UP** TO **HEAVEN** WHILE **HE** WAS **STILL ALIVE.**

The power verification of Elisha proves his lineage to Elisha. It's the public identification of the private practice. The sons of the prophets came and showed honor to Elisha when he demonstrated the Spirit was with him. Where is our demonstration? It sets up our words to be recognized as the language of Heaven in the Earth. When we follow the protocol of the prophetic lineage, it invites those who would come to us to carry our torch into their generation.

PROPHETIC LINEAGE

To apprehend all that God has for us in the story, we must align ourselves with proper context. When the question is asked, "Where is the Lord the God of Elijah?", It regards Elijah's identity as a prophet. Elisha knew who Elijah as a Prophet to the nation and knew his place in relationship to Elijah. In asking the question, Elisha both activates and reveals his prophetic lineage. He positions himself to receive the answer before he asks the question. We are "shooting ourselves in the dark" if we ask the question before we position ourselves as Elisha did. The answer to this question often goes unanswered because those asking are not in alignment with the spirit of Elijah. They desire an answer before they understand the question—what they're asking for—and the placement necessary to capture the response.

Elisha follows the protocol Elijah set for him to succeed. Elijah's plan all along was to pass the torch to Elisha and the coming generations, which is the essence of the spirit of Elijah. It's a continuation of what God is doing on the Earth. The answer to the question comes when we position ourselves in the lineage. In the Sky Dream, I tracked with the wisdom of the prophet. I stayed by his side. Elisha stayed connected to Elijah. Family is key to inheritance. Stay close to Jesus, and you position yourself to receive everything Jesus desires to give you—or you unlock everything He has already given you. The torch passes to all who believe.

THREE PARADIGMS

The Family was united and aware. The precipice of the spectacular was in the air as the day they all were waiting for arrived. Everyone knew that this day would be unique. Elijah knew it, his spiritual son knew it, and the sons of the prophets knew it. There was nervous excitement, anticipation, and expectation gripping the hearts of each one.

We already imagined what Elijah himself must've been thinking, but what about Elisha? What was going through his mind? He too lived his whole life to ascend this moment. A complex variety of emotions probably flooded his soul. Today he would lose his father, yet gain new sons and daughters. He is graduating one way of life and inaugurating another. It is the joy of becoming what you've been dreaming about coupled with the sorrow of being separated from your dearest companion.

Paradigm three is one of the sons of the prophets. They would watch their two fathers of the faith—their spiritual heroes—combine for an encounter of the ages, and witness the torch of the Lord pass from one generation to another.

Each player had different, yet important roles. If we consider the bigger picture, we will discover the depth this encounter provides. The storyline is not singular; it's a three-dimensional experience: Elijah's view, Elisha's view, and the prophets' view. If we keep this in mind as we read through the story, the whole picture will begin to take shape.

ELISHA'S DOUBLE PORTION

The day started with a journey through a few cities. In each city, the sons of the prophets came to greet them. They all seemed to know "what was up." When they entered a new city, Elijah asked Elisha to stay behind, as the Lord was sending him further. Elisha knew this was the day they'd been waiting for, and he would not be content to stay behind and say goodbye, he would journey with his father until they reached the moment of realization.

Elijah's final destination was the river Jordan. The company of prophets watched from a distance as the waters parted and they crossed over. Next, Elisha's persistence pays off when Elijah asks him what he can do for him before he is taken away.

> When they had crossed over, Elijah said to Elisha, 'Ask what I shall do for you before I am taken from you.' And Elisha said, 'Please, let a double portion of your spirit be upon me.' He said, 'You have asked a hard

thing. Nevertheless, if you see me when I am taken from you, it shall be so for you; but if not, it shall not be so.'

vv 2:9-10

WHY!? Why did Elijah have to see him taken to inherit the "double portion?" This riddle perplexed me. I wasn't content to merely read it; I needed to know why it had to happen this way. Remember, everything in this story was happening on purpose. Elisha had to follow Elijah until he asked what he wanted as his inheritance. This moment would be pivotal for receiving the mantle and the calling as the Prophet of a new generation in Israel.

On a quest to discover the answer, I inserted myself into the story and began to play a part in it centuries later. By putting myself in Elisha's shoes, I viewed the requirement of seeing Elijah ascend like a giant mystery—inviting me to come inside and have a look around. The answer didn't arrive instantly, as it became a journey of several years. What was the secret to seeing Elijah ascend to Heaven that was crucial for Elisha to receive his inheritance?

One of the first things I discovered was that to know why Elijah answered Elisha's question the way that he did, we must clarify what Elisha was asking.

In modern Pentecostal and Charismatic circles, many try to recreate this scenario in their own lives, based on their paradigm of what they think the passage means. For example, there are those go from place-to-place and minister-to-minister, asking them all for a "double portion" of whatever miracles, supernatural gifts, talents, finances, etc. present in the person's life. Most instances include the seeker asking someone in whom they admire, such as a pastor or a prophet, to pray for them or lay hands on them, so they receive the same mantle of power and anointing.

While I do not entirely invalidate this, many miss what was happening in the story because they've found a formula to follow.

Asking for a mantle is like asking Superman for his cape. If you get the cape, it doesn't automatically mean you can fly. Elisha had the cape, but also demonstrated he had the power behind the cape. The cape or mantle is an outward symbol of inward power. On the outside, Elisha got a new cloak, but on the inside, he received new authority, calling, and power. I do believe in visualizing, and in some cases, reenacting Biblical principles, but if we aren't careful, we will follow a formula yet miss the connecting to God.

Many now use this story as a Biblical precedent for receiving double portions from people. Not only do they want superman's cape, but they also want one that is twice as powerful.

Is this possible?

In one sense I feel that the term "double portion" is overused and abused. I admit that I used to ask for double portions as well. On the other hand, we should be inspired by our Biblical heroes and long to walk with God the way they do. I am sure that Elisha felt this way. Elijah was his father and hero. He was the one in whom he looked up to and wanted to be like the most. I wanted to be like them both, which is the reason behind my search of the "WHY?".

Another misunderstanding I've seen regarding the double portion is from the perspective of the one giving the mantle. Elijah was the giver, and Elisha was the receiver. Elijah had a plan of inheritance for Elisha. It wasn't just a one-time prayer. Many "givers" have recognized this, but misapplied it. I have heard people say that when someone asks them for a double portion that they feel sorry for them because of all that they had gone through to attain to the "level" of revelation and anointing. This kind of mentality also misses the point of the story. You can receive something without having to do what the other person did to get it. Elijah blazed a trail for Elisha to walk in; he didn't have to start over and carve a new path through the jungle. Elijah gave the gear needed to keep the trail going.

With these schools of thought in view, we will now open up the passage from a different angle. I feel the above interpretations can be expanded by adding another line to the equation.

Dr. Michael L. Brown, president of FIRE School of Ministry, of which I am an alumnus, describes in his book *From Holy Laughter to Holy Fire*, that Elijah wanted the inheritance of the firstborn.

> According to Deuteronomy 21:15-17, if a man had two sons, instead of splitting the inheritance fifty-fifty, he had to divide it into three parts, giving two thirds to the firstborn (the "double portion") and one third to the second born son. Most people have mistakenly believed that the double portion meant "twice as much"; it simply means "double share."
>
> So what's the big deal? It's a matter of spiritual realism. We can't give something we don't have naturally or spiritually. We can't impart double anointings.[1]

The primary emphasis that I perceive Brown points out here is that this passage does not refer to someone laying hands on you, and you instantly receiving twice as much anointing as the person praying for you. It is a share of the inheritance. Instead of one share, he wanted double–the right of a firstborn.

So, what does this "share" consist of? What was Elisha to receive as an inheritance, besides an old coat? Walter Brueggemann, in his commentary on the Books of Kings, gives some illustration:

> ...Elijah grants Elisha one last wish. His request is bold and prompt, a "double share" of Elijah's spirit. The "double share" is one more portion than is normally distributed. The phrasing is odd because "double share" refers to something quantifiable, but Elijah asked for rûah, for the force and vitality, energy and authority of Elijah, none of which is quantifiable. He asked to be invested with Elijah's power as a prophet.[2]

Elisha's request is an inheritance of the Spirit. He wanted a double share of that which was on Elijah, the same way a firstborn son would receive a double share of the natural inheritance. Remembering who Elijah was and the power in his life reveals the significance of Elisha receiving his mantle to become the new prophetic voice to Israel—walking in even greater power than Elijah. If Elijah couldn't give something greater, or twice as much as he had to Elisha, then how was this possible for Elisha to do twice as many miracles as Elijah? He had to be present when Elijah left, so he could continue where Elijah left off.

ELIJAH'S LIFE WAS A **LIFE** OF **ENCOUNTERS.**
HE **COMMANDED** THE **HEAVENS** TO **WITHHOLD RAIN** FOR YEARS
BEFORE **ALLOWING** THEM TO **OPEN AGAIN.**
HE **RAISED** THE **DEAD.**
THE SPIRIT **TRANSPORTED** HIM.
HE **CALLED FIRE DOWN** FROM **HEAVEN.**
BREAKFAST-MAKING ANGELS VISITED HIM.
HE HAD **NUMEROUS ENCOUNTERS** WITH THE **WORD** OF THE
LORD.
HE **SAW** THE **LORD PASS BY.**
HE **EXPERIENCED** THE **WIND BREAKING ROCKS** INTO **PIECES,**
THE **FEELING** OF THE **EARTH SHAKING** UNDER HIS FEET, THE
FIRE OF GOD, AND THE **WHISPER OF INTIMACY** WITH HIS
HEAVENLY FATHER.

He experienced miracle after miracle and encounter after encounter. It was all building toward something. It was all part of Heaven's divine design to reveal Yahweh to Israel through the life of a man, which would culminate in one final, awesome, and all-encompassing encounter. The subsequent encounter would be the height of his ministry. It would be the event in which all of the other encounters were both preparing him for and guiding him towards.

Elijah would not die; he was going to ascend into Heaven while still alive, which would be the culmination of his life. Enoch is the only other person in canonical Scripture—other than Jesus Himself—to experience an encounter like this.

The wake of Elijah's ministry was massive. It would affect the entire planet for every single generation to follow him. There had to be a legacy. There had to be someone to continue the miracles, the encounters, and the ministry of Yahweh to Israel. As we know, the someone was Elisha. Elijah and Elisha did life together. They were a family. They encountered God together, and they would experience Elijah's ascension together. Elisha experienced Elijah's ministry and relationship with God, and then he began his own.

THE CULMINATION IS A GENERATIONAL TRANSFER.

It is Father's desire for his plan to continue from generation to generation. Family is designed to continue, expand, and fulfill.

In order for this transfer happen, Elisha had to be present at Elijah's ascension. He had to be there to witness the culminating encounter if he was going to receive the double-share inheritance and pass the torch of the Lord to a new generation.

EXPERIENCE THE ENCOUNTER

Elijah needed to be there at the precise moment Heaven opened up and escorted Elijah into its courts. He had to see it, to hear it, to smell, taste it, and feel it. His heart, his soul, and his spirit had to examine it, to know it, and to feast on it.

It was as if this was a heavenly door of unlimited revelation and supernatural atomic power that he had to walk through to get to the inheritance. If he did not see it, he would not have everything that I just described as part of his life's history. He would've been a remarkable prophet, for sure. But he wouldn't have been the Elisha that we read about.

From this moment onward, he was the one living person who could:

RECITE WHAT THE **WIND** OF **HEAVEN SOUNDS LIKE,**
WHAT THE **FIRE** OF **HEAVEN FEELS LIKE,**
AND WHAT THE **BELLY** OF **HEAVEN LOOKS LIKE.**

The "separation" of Heaven and Earth uncloaked in front of him. His whole body experienced it. An exponential experience baptized him. He became the living embodiment of the encounter. The record of the encounter rewired his DNA.

Just as it took a lifetime for Elijah to come to the place of his ascension into Heaven—a lifetime to attain to that "level" of revelation—it was vital for Elisha to see him and experience the revelation with him, so Elisha could start where Elijah left off. Elijah's ministry culminated with the same revelation that inaugurated Elisha's ministry.

THE ASCENDED LIFESTYLE

Witnesses of ascension receive the power of ascension: Elisha and Elisha, the disciples and Jesus, us and Holy Spirit. There is a massive focus on the crucifixion of Jesus, moderate focus on the resurrection of Jesus, but little focus on the ascension of Jesus.

THE **ASCENDED LIFESTYLE** IS THE **ONE** WHICH **BRINGS HEAVEN TO EARTH.**

If my friend is playing a video game and gets to level 50, then stops and says, "it's your turn," I don't have to start back at level one. Even though he did all the work, I get to start at level 50. Elisha saw Elijah ascend. Therefore, he was able to start right where Elijah left off, just as if it were Elijah continuing in his ministry. Elijah's "ceiling" became Elisha's "floor." Elijah and Elisha were proximate to each other through doing life together. When we are proximate to the ascended Jesus by spending time with Him in the secret place, we gain access to everything He has access to (Eph 2:6). We are the beneficiary of His ascent into the higher levels because of our closeness to Him. Proximity to Jesus is a life spent with Him.

His presence is everywhere, yet many are unaware and fail to engage, to relate, to speak, or to listen. Elisha wasn't a drone, nor was he a clone. Having his own personality, he chose to become Family with Elijah. This relationship granted him access to all that the Family had to offer. Jesus, even in His newfound human form, still only did what He saw His Father doing. He demonstrated true Sonship. The disciples followed the protocol set before them. They related to Jesus just as Jesus related to His Father. His goal was for His disciples to multiply His legacy and outshine Him.

While meditating on these things one day at a church meeting, the Lord gave me a prophetic word for a friend. I described to her how God was going to use her to do things in the Spirit. She would journey into the depths of God as others before her, but she would retain the fine details, which many overlook, because of the complexity of the encounter. Her perception was like a new technology in which she could function in her prophetic gifting with updated software. Whereas they were shocked by the encounter alone, she was able to "take stock" and become a gateway for others to engage the depths of Heaven.

Over the course of life, God reveals things to people. In the ministry of the Kingdom, we are essentially sharing the revelations God shows us with the people in our lives. These may be things that have taken our whole lives to comprehend. The cool thing is that we did not just do it for ourselves. The entire body benefits from sharing. Others can take our revelation and run with it. Strength builds when we are in fellowship with one another. As our experiences merge, we cover more ground more quickly and transform the Earth with the presence of God.

I spent over a decade of prayer and study for the revelation in this chapter. Although it took me more than ten years, the beauty of the Kingdom is that it may only take you the time you spend reading it. We freely give what we have been freely given. I benefit my wife by spending my life with her, but I benefit you by sharing this book with you. Likewise, you benefit those around you through varying spheres of influence, relationships, and mediums.

GENERATIONAL TRANSFIGURATION

Elisha knew that now was the time for him to walk in the prophetic call of God on his life. Now was the time for him to be the prophet to his generation. The question, "Where is the Lord the God of Elijah?" was also an announcement. He was effectively stating,

"HERE IS THE LORD, THE GOD OF ELIJAH!"

He already knew God, but now he was stepping into his call, replacing Elijah as a prophetic light and voice of Israel. God was present within him just as He was present with Elijah.

His walk through the waters of the Jordan River birthed his ministry. It had to be supernatural if it was to reveal that he carried the same power and spirit as Elijah. He called upon the God to part the waters just as his father had only a few moments ago. Elisha received the mantle that the Lord placed on Elijah and would now relate to God in a whole new way. Elisha's mission was to fulfill Elijah's mandate and launch his call. He used Elijah's torch to light up his path. He didn't ignore what his father had done; he embraced it.

Elijah ended strong, and Elisha would now start strong. Transference is the essence of the hearts of the fathers turning to the children and the children to the fathers. A "generational transfer" is how we so often hear it explained. However, I would call it a generational transfiguration. Each generation has more revelation than the previous generation in light of the understanding of the knowledge of God for the unfolding of the times. Therefore, when this revelation passes from generation to generation, there is a multiplying of powers, not just addition. The clearer it gets and the further it unfolds, more of God's plan for the ages is visible to us.

IT IS A **METAMORPHOSIS** FROM **ONE GENERATION** TO THE **NEXT.**

It is as if the generations progress from caterpillar to butterfly to blue jay to eagle. Each generation transforms or transfigures into something beyond. It is like a circle that expands twice its size as it spirals upward through the years, with each heart catapulting it higher and higher.

> Behold I am going to send you Elijah the prophet before the coming great and terrible day of the Lord. He will restore the hearts of the fathers to the children and the hearts of the children to the fathers, so that I will not come and smite the land with a curse.

> Malachi 4:5-6 NASB

Now we know according to the Gospel of Matthew that Jesus declared John the Baptist as Elijah who was to come (v 11:14). Elijah was a forerunner of Jesus, which is why John the Baptist embodied the continuation of the ministry of Elijah and the transfer to Elisha, so would he transfer to Jesus. Many believe Elijah will himself return as one of the two witnesses mentioned in the book of Revelation. That may be true, but I believe there is a generational fulfillment present as well. We need mentors and parents who take their knowledge of God and pour the substance of that wisdom into the young ones around them. Also, the young ones need to embrace and learn from them without trying to do it all on their own.

THE GENERATIONS MUST COME TOGETHER FOR THE WORLD TO SEE A TRUE PICTURE OF WHO OUR GOD REALLY IS.

The church is a Family, and as such should have as its priority the welfare of her kids.

The Father's heart is to raise up each new generation as Family.

116

REVIVALS OFTEN STOP BECAUSE THE GENERATIONS ARE AT ODDS WITH EACH OTHER.

This cycle leaves the "rebellious" younger generation starting over instead of picking up where the "stubborn" older generation left off. When the generations finally come together, the world will shake. Imagine an entire generation of Elijahs raising up an entire generation of Elishas!

MODELS?

Elijah is a father of the faith. He walked in the power of God when he was on the Earth, and now he walks in the presence of God in Heaven. His legacy is a prototype model for all fathers of the faith.

Today we need fathers and mothers who walk in the power and inheritance Elijah, full of the Holy Spirit, and who know God. Revival continues when the matriarchs and patriarchs take their place and nurture a generation.

> And it shall come about in the last days, God says; "That I will pour out my Spirit on all mankind; and your sons and your daughters shall prophesy, and your young men shall see visions and your old men will dream dreams: Even on my bondslaves, both men and women, I will in those days pour forth My Spirit, and they shall prophesy.
>
> Acts 2:17-18 NASB

Amazingly, this was Peter's explanation for the drunk-like state of those baptized in the Spirit on the day of Pentecost. He stood with the disciples

117

as fathers to translate the heavenly wonder of the experience. These "drunken beings" became models of supernatural splendor in their generation, just as Elijah and Elisha. The willingness to model a supernatural life may draw criticism from those with earthbound thinking, but it is a necessity to see the generations transcend.

The demarcation that we are children of God is manifest when we are full of the Spirit and walking in the power of the Spirit. We need models to look up to that walk in the Spirit like this, and we need to become models for those in our midst. Where are the Elijahs of God?

THE MANTLE

In viewing the coming of the Holy Spirit on the Day of Pentecost through the story of Elijah and Elisha, Jesus showed me a new angle to perceive His ascension and why He sent His Spirit. He was tracking with and expanding the trajectory of the spirit of Elijah. Elijah had a school of the prophets and Jesus had a school of apostles. When Jesus was about to ascend into Heaven, he also gathered his disciples, His Elisha generation to him.

> For John baptized with water, but you will be baptized with the Holy Spirit not many days from now... but you will receive power when the Holy Spirit has come upon you; and you shall be My witnesses both in Jerusalem, and in all Judea and Samaria, and even to the remotest part of the earth. And after He had said these things, He was lifted up while they were looking on, and a cloud received Him out of their sight.

> Acts 1:5, 1:8-9 NASB

The disciples saw Jesus ascend to Heaven and were instructed to go to Jerusalem and wait for the baptism of the Holy Spirit. They were to await their mantle. The same way that Elijah left Elisha his mantle, Jesus was sending the Holy Spirit (Mantle) to His disciples.

After Elisha had received Elijah's mantle, the sons of the prophets declared "The spirit of Elijah rests on Elisha," (2 Ki 2:15). They recognized the same anointing. Peter and John tasted a similar experience:

> Now as they observed the confidence of Peter and John and understood that they were uneducated and untrained men, they were amazed, and began to recognize them as having been with Jesus.

> Acts 4:13 NASB

Just as the revelation did not leave with Elijah, neither did it leave with Jesus. Both left their mantles to the next generation. What the disciples had spent the last few years of their lives watching Jesus do, he was now empowering them to do. And not only that, He was calling them to do even greater things because now they would have full capacity to relate to Him in the Holy Spirit.

Their foundation and starting place was everything they had seen Jesus do. They were to inherit a double portion as well. They would begin at the exact point Jesus left off. This was their platform of influence. Just like Elisha, they would directly continue all that He started.

Jesus transfigured just before his Passion. He lit up like lightning in front of Peter, James, and John. Peter's first instinct was to camp there, living in only what Jesus was doing. Instead, Jesus kept moving. He showed them what they were to become when baptized in the Holy Spirit.

TRANSCENDENCE: THE ENCOUNTER THAT SIGNALED THE CONCLUSION OF JESUS' EARTHLY MINISTRY WAS TO BE THE ONE TO SIGNAL THE BEGINNING OF THE DISCIPLES' MINISTRY.

Elijah's discoveries in Heaven became the mantles he left on the Earth. Jesus came from Heaven in a demonstration of power. When He returned, He sent the same power of the Holy Spirit to the Earth. This mantle is available to YOU! They recognized the same spirit that was on Elijah was also on Elisha. They recognized that Peter and John were like Jesus! What will they recognize on you? On us? On our generation? Where are the Elijahs of God? Is it you? What does it look like when Heaven comes down? It looks like us because Heaven is our mantle!

ACTIVATION

Heaven is available. It is open for encounters. You are invited in. Take some time to soak in God's presence. Tell Him you are ready. He has a personal encounter waiting for you.

What did you experience in your encounter?

Now, think about how this encounter ties into your history with God, and how it unlocks your destiny with God?

How can you use this encounter to enhance the way those in your life experience God?

DECLARATION

I will wear the mantle of the supernatural in my generation. I will become a son... a daughter... a father... a mother... I will be both a receiver and a giver. I will function as both an Elijah, and as an Elisha to my generation. I will honor my parents, protect their legacy, and provide an inheritance for my kids. I will freely give my mantle to future generations.

RISE REVIVALISTS!

NOTES

[1] Dr. Michael L. Brown, *From Holy Laughter to Holy Fire; America on the Edge of Revival,* (Shippensburg, Destiny Image1996), 155-156.
[2] Walter Brueggemann, *Smyth & Helwys Bible Commentary; 1 & 2 Kings,* (Macon, Smyth & Helwys Publishing, INC 2000), 295.

SIX

REVIVALS & REVIVALISTS

"I THINK YOU HAVE THE POWER!"

One summer, my wife and I were vacationing in St. Augustine, FL. We were looking for a parking space so we could walk around the old downtown. I found a spot on the street, but I was a little hesitant to park there because it was next to a terminal that required a fee. Finally, I figured this was as good as any, so I parked the car, then got out and walked over to the machine to pay.

Suddenly, a homeless man ran over to me and said, "You don't have to pay that." I replied in frustration as I asked, "Why not!" "Because it's after 5:00 pm," he explained. "After 5:00 you don't have to pay." Relieved, I thanked him for warning me before I unnecessarily donated five bucks to good ole' St. Augustine.

We struck up a conversation in which he told me he was on disability. Well, this made me just as angry as being bothered a few moments earlier. "Why are you on disability!?" I asked as I interrupted him. "Because of my back and hip," he replied. He went on to describe the issues in more detail, but by then I'd had enough. This gentleman went out of his way to help me when he didn't even have a place to lay his head. I was upset with the affliction the enemy was using to keep him from enjoying life.

I interrupted his story and said, "Let me pray for you." He said "okay," so I put my hand on his shoulder and began to declare God's power over him. I spoke to his back and hips, telling them to do what they were created to do!

I felt nothing but frustration, yet I knew that God was going to touch him. God moves in the midst of wherever we are at in life. The moments we may feel the least qualified are often moments of breakthrough.

After speaking life to his body, I asked him how he felt. Nonchalantly, he answered, "the same." His response caught me off guard. Even though I was frustrated, I still expected God to touch him right then.

He continued talking for about 30 more seconds. Suddenly, he stops and looks at me, with his eyes wide open. "Hey man, I think you have power," he said, "cause my hip don't hurt anymore." He put his hand on his lower back and hip as he said this indicating that the area that was now pain-free.

I said, "That's the Holy Ghost!" He answered back, "Yeah I know, other people have prayed for me too, and it didn't work."

He was hurting. He needed a heavenly touch. He needed a son or a daughter of God to reveal the love of Jesus to him in power. His need went beyond, "I'll keep you in my prayers." His need was of the moment. God had all the other parking spaces in St. Augustine full that day, so we would park where we did so we could love-on this man and heal his body. God didn't see my frustration at the parking situation and abort his plan. He used it. All things work together for the good of those who are in Christ Jesus (Romans 8:25). Next time you are having "one of those days," stay alert. God may be setting you up to touch someone.

His initial reaction indicated that he thought the prayer would be powerless. He appreciated the fact that I was willing to pray for him, but there was almost zero expectation that anything would happen, which is why his eyes looked like a "deer in headlights" when Jesus touched him.

When he exclaimed, "I think you have the power!", it was an amazing kiss from Heaven in his life. He had a history of well-meaning people loving him in the midst of his life, yet praying powerless prayers. They were able to provide love, but not power. Both are essential. My love tank was lacking in the moment, but the power was not. Leif Hetland says that we need to know "when to be love, when to be power, and when to be wisdom." All the prayers before were not entirely irrelevant as they were key to opening up his heart to receive prayer when someone asked.

Pursue love, and earnestly desire the spiritual gifts...

1 Corinthians 14:1a

Stories like this allow for connection to the amazing testimonies of God moving through people both in the Bible and in church history. I used my account as a place of introduction and first-hand experience. God has always used His people to ignite revivals. In this chapter, we will glean from a few of those revivals and the revivalists who sparked them.

First off, if we study recent or even ancient moves of God, there is an interesting observation particularly in the effects of youth and revival. Many revivalists had radical encounters at early ages.

Charles Fox Parham encountered Jesus at the age of 13, held his first public meeting at 15, and had his first evangelist meeting at 18. Before that meeting, he went up on a hillside, and stretched his hands out over the valley, to engage Heaven in prayer that the whole community "be taken for God."[1]

Parham's influence quickly began to grow over the next few years and attract those desiring training for the ministry. He opened a Bible school in Topeka, Kansas, at Stone's Folly. Iconically, they named the school Bethel. They began experiencing manifestations of healing and revelation of God's Kingdom, which led Parham to give his students the assignment of discovering the evidence of the Baptism of the Spirit according to Scripture.

After a few days of study and prayer, they concluded that every recipient of the Baptism spoke in other tongues. His students began to pray for the experience. God answered as many were overcome in his presence and spoke in tongues. An outpouring of the Spirit erupted, and newspapers began reporting "A New Pentecost." Word of the movement spread and by 1902 Parham had become known as the "Father of Pentecost."

AZUSA STREET REVIVAL

Later, Parham moved to Houston, Texas and launched a new school. One of his students and spiritual sons there was William Seymour, who would go on to become the leader of the 1906 Azusa Street Revival in Los Angeles, CA. During this time, God moved powerfully through Seymour. At the revival, they would spend hours in the presence, little children would play in the glory, and many signs and wonders took place. As thousands upon thousands visited from all parts of the globe, this revival spread the Pentecostal movement around the world.

Seymour was the leader and catalyst of the revival, but his inheritance flowed through Parham. What we have today in Pentecostal and Charismatic Christianity can, at least in part, be credited to a young man—Parham—who had encounters with God even as a teenager. He took these encounters as his arsenal to raise up his generation in an aspect of God that had been relatively hidden since the Great Awakenings.

PARHAM'S ENCOUNTERS WERE HIS ARSENAL.

Seymour then amplified the message of Parham, taking it to the next level. Although Parham and Seymour would later drift apart, there was a generational transfer that saw the revival in Topeka ignite in LA, and ultimately spread across the globe.

WELSH REVIVAL

Another way the Azusa outpouring impacted the world was through the outpouring of the Spirit. Writer and evangelist, Frank Bartleman, who joined Seymour in California, was a correspondent of Evan Roberts, the leader of another revival that started in Wales two years earlier. From 1904-1905, the entire nation of Wales was impacted by this revival, as the Spirit of God moved mightily. A conservative number of those saved is 150,000. Azusa pulled from two streams—Parham and Roberts—and created a tidal wave that swept across the planet.

I mentioned the Azusa Revival before the Welsh Revival, even though it happened after because it is the link between Topeka and Wales. Seeing how things flow together grants us—as students of history—the ability to see the pattern of God as he moves across the earth. At the turn of the century, communication was quicker than it had ever been. News of moves of God traveled fast, which is how these two revival streams became one in Azusa and transformed the spiritual climate of the world.

The Welsh Revival is one of my favorites in church history. I dive deep into it once or twice per year. This revival rebooted a nation. I don't know if you have been to Europe, particularly the UK, but soccer is a big deal, both now, and 100 years ago. The presence of God so draped over the nation that even the matches stopped for a season, not because they were wrong, but because people were just so in love with God that they spent their time gathering together in worship. Also, bars closed, the police had to shift from fighting crime to crowd control, families restored, and miners had to retrain their donkeys because they commanded them by using curse words.

EVAN ROBERTS

At 13 years of age, young Evan began to experience significant encounters with God. Growing up, he gained a reputation for being "deeply spiritual." The culture of Wales was Christian, so it wasn't taboo for someone to have strong Biblical values. Evan, however, was different. Jesus consumed his life. He had a vision that God wanted to save 100 thousand people in Wales.

> Because of his unique desire for the Lord, Evan gave himself to fervent prayer and intercession, that by the time he was twenty years old, he was known by some as a "mystical lunatic."[2]

The revival began one day when he got permission to share after the church service with a few people about his hunger for God to move. As he shared his encounters, hunger ensued in the people to experience God themselves. People left the meeting changed, wanting nothing but God. Word spread like a fire that God was on the move. It quickly tapped into a vein of expectancy that revival was coming to Wales. Within six weeks, Evan's vision for 100 thousand souls became a reality.

History is born in the heart of the hungry. Once again, we have a young person so on fire for God that he impacted his friends, his nation, the entire world, and future generations. His legacy is that he chose to love God above everything else. His friends even described him as:

"A **PARTICLE** OF **RADIUM** WHOSE **FIRE** IN THEIR **MIDST** WAS CONSUMING."

Does your heart burn like mine when reading such incredible stories? Do you want to burn like Evan Roberts? I do! I want to be known as "a particle of radium whose fire is consuming." Who uses words like this to describe a human being? It sounds like the way the comics describe superheroes! I want to be around those who are whose lives are satisfied in God. I want everything I do to burn with the fires of Heaven. Does this make you burn as I do? Can we, together, join in the legacy of Evan's burning? Let's grab the mantle and charge ahead!

History recalls Evan as burning one in public because he lit the fire when no one was looking. For a season, just before the revival broke out, he would pray at night and be taken to heaven from 1 am to 3 am- every night.

WE CANNOT **BRING HEAVEN TO EARTH** UNLESS **WE** HAVE **BEEN TO HEAVEN.**

SALVATION IS **SUPPOSED** TO **BE A BRAND NEW HEAVENLY LIFE,** NOT **JUST** A **RENEWED EARTHLY ONE.**

Evan's heavenly life surged past the point of equilibrium and spilled out into his public life as revival poured out on his nation.

> When you pray, go into your inner room, close your door
> and pray to your Father who is in secret, and your Father
> who sees what is done in secret will reward you.
>
> Matthew 6:6 NASB

REVIVALS ARE **BORN** LIKE **BUTTERFLIES.**
SOMEONE SOMEWHERE **ENTERS METAMORPHOSIS.**

There was first a secret life. If the cocoon is the caterpillar's prayer closet, then the butterfly is the revival that happens in its life. Revivalists didn't start movements; they burned for God in such a way that a movement began to flow through them. In secret, they set a wick on fire that just happened to light an atomic bomb in Heaven that rained His presence down on Earth.

HEBRIDES REVIVAL

Along with the Welsh Revival, the Hebrides Revival is one that I glean from the most. Fortunately, this revival was mid-century, and we have some first-hand accounts still available, which adds dimension because we get to hear not just from historians, but from the people themselves.

The revival that occurred in Scotland in 1949. The Hebrides are a small group of islands off the northwest coast. There was a certain level of expectancy for a move of God among the islands, which came to a flash-point on the Isle of Lewis. There was "great concern that the church had become powerless to hold young people," and a plea went out to pray for the youth. The Smith sisters, who were two ladies in their eighties, answered the call. They began to pray for "water to be poured out on dry and thirsty land." I imagine their intercession as them hitting Heaven like a piñata until it burst. A particular verse that stirred their hearts and the hearts of others was Psalm 24:

> Who shall ascend the hill of the LORD? And who shall
> stand in his holy place? He who has clean hands and a
> pure heart, who does not lift up his soul to what is false
> and does not swear deceitfully. He will receive blessing
> from the LORD and righteousness from the God of his

salvation. Such is the generation of those who seek him, who seek the face of the God of Jacob.

vv 3-6 ESV

They also prayed for someone who knew God in a deep way to come to the island. A couple of weeks later, Duncan Campbell arrived for a two-week meeting. He ended up staying three years because revival took root. After his first meeting, a few folks stayed to pray. In the early morning hours, the presence of God swooped into the community. Those who lived close to the church came out of their houses saturated in the "awareness of God." Strange and awesome things began to happen.

Rather than tell you, I have assembled some quotes about the revival from those who experienced it firsthand:

And suddenly he was aware that something was happening inside him.

Neil MacArthur

God asked his people to ask Him a question, 'Will you come and visit us?' And He said, 'Yes, I will,' and He did.

Alistair Petrie

It went out to the whole community. Everybody felt it. It didn't matter whether they were Christians or not.

Donald John Smith

People walking down the road would hear the singing, and they would know that the people were revived because of the life in the singing.

Katie Campbell

There was something in the singing, something as if it just came down from heaven, there was... you couldn't describe it... there's something in the singing you can't hear from an ordinary person.

Donald John Smith

One night a certain man was praying and he was seeing a white dove resting on people's heads... and they were all converted that night.

Donald John Smith

But the ones that were lying on the floor there, you would see Christ on their face. You would know that they were with Jesus, for their face was just shining, just shining it was!

Donald John Smith

Day and night, whenever you woke up, the presence of the Lord was there. When you went to your bed, the presence of the Lord was there.

Donald John Smith

However, they have also encountered God as this blast from heaven, this incredible surge of power.

Alistair Petrie

One of the houses shook in Arnol there... as when they were praying, the house shook.

Donald John Smith

Before we had maybe minutes of it. But then we had hours of it.

Donald John Smith

Whether it's a house that shakes with prayer or whether it's light coming out of the skies like electricity...

Alistair Petrie

Whether you see this profound divinity coming as a Gospel Ship — which a whole lot of them saw at one point... And they all saw this ship which has been seen only a few times in history, so I'm told.

Alistair Petrie

Another night as we left we saw in the open fields a ship, as if it was a navy ship, all lit up, all lit up between the masts and everything. But we knew it wasn't real, but... for it was on dry land. We couldn't say a word. None of us could even speak. 'Be still and know that I am God.' That's all we could say.

Donald John Smith

Crowds walking down the road... lights would be 'round them. They would be surrounded by lights.

Donald John Smith

Ships passing by felt the presence of the Lord... They felt the presence of the Lord, even going around the island.

Donald John Smith

There's been a revival here in [the] 20's, the 30's... it's as if the promise of each generation was then passed on to the next generation. And something of the nature of God is; He knows who He can count on to test the promises, to be a trip wire of change, and suddenly release the promises of God into the present generation.

Alistair Petrie

And I think the prayers of these that have passed on are now being answered, it's not just the prayers of the present.

Neil MacArthur

There's a new wave of young people who have no embarrassment about praying, no embarrassment about coming together.

Alistair Petrie

He then takes the fruit of that encounter. And it's like He sends it to all the world... He says this is what it's like if people will come and spend time, even on their knees; and they will meet with Me. I will meet with them.

Alistair Petrie

I don't believe it's God's heart for us to be complacent—that He really does want us to live in revival.

Katie Campbell

God's just about to release His glory in our lives again!

Alistair Petrie relaying what the
Hebrides Islanders told him

How amazing! These quotes are from a video about the revival produced by Sentinel Group.3 We could dissect each quote and explore the glory of God it reveals, but I will let them inspire you into your encounters. Their testimonies paint a picture that extends beyond commonplace accounts of revival. They would be walking through the fields, from meeting to meeting, and look up to see the heavens literally open. The hungry hearts of the elderly Smith sisters were kindred to the youthful heart of Evan Roberts. All of them became igniters of revival for their generation.

THE ORACLE

To unlock the depths of the Hebridean Revival would take volumes by itself. I've listened to messages by Duncan Campbell about the revival, and you can hear the essence—the Spirit—of revival resonating in the sound of his voice. Here is a phrase he commonly used to describe the revival:

"A **STRANGE CONSCIOUSNESS** OF **GOD** HAD **GRIPPED** THE **COMMUNITY**."

What fantastic language! Words like this are only produced in presence. He doesn't just tell you a story, he speaks as an oracle. I am so moved when I hear him because it awakens the voice—the oracle—deep inside of me. The ones who unlock this are the ones who recite Heaven on Earth. As you read, I decree that these words will awaken and activate the oracle inside of you.

Each generation is designed to build upon the previous generation and lay a foundation for the next generation. Eric Johnson illustrates this in excellence his book, *Momentum*. The testimonies of the saints of the Isle of Lewis who experienced this cosmic move of God are signposts to guide us into our own revival encounters. These kinds of experiences are available for us today. If you take God out of the box of religious misunderstanding, you will find that He is painting a wonderful, creative, and amazing canvas.

STEAMS OF GLORY

There are many wonderful stories of the glory of God manifesting all-throughout church history, just as in Topeka, Azusa, Wales, and Lewis. I was also privileged to experience the manifest glory during my time at the Brownsville Revival.

Once, during the worship time at one of the revival services, the Spirit of God was rich, and all the people were either kneeling or lying prostrate in awe of His presence. I, on-the-other-hand, was having a natural encounter and exited to use the restroom. I mused on the significant increase of God's presence I felt this night, but I was unprepared for what was about to happen. When I opened the door to go back into the sanctuary, I could barely see the platform. There was a misty glory cloud all across the front of the auditorium. If you have ever turned on the hot water in your shower and then left while it was still running, you know that when you return, the room would be full of steam. What I saw was like this, but multiplied. Its appearance was as if there were one-hundred showers going full blast with super-hot water pouring out. Just imagine all the steam that would generate.

I heard similar stories of the glory of God appearing at the Revival, but this was the first time I encountered it. I had often dreamed of seeing it. The stories filled me with the hope that it would soon happen. Now, the table was set for me to dine in the desires of my heart. This encounter awakened the experience in my life. Afterward, I knew that the glory rested there, and I expected to see it again. I knew when to look for it and how the Spirit of God was moving. Sometimes in a service, I would look up and see a small white cloud resting in the pinnacle of the roof or around the platform. I didn't stop at the initial encounter; I began to steward my spiritual perception. I wanted to see all the glory I could. As I retell these encounters, I am so grateful for the season of glory I was able to experience at the Brownsville Revival.

My most intense encounter with the glory cloud came a year later in a worship service at Fire School of Ministry. I was dancing wildly as the drum circle called out the warrior in me. I closed my eyes and lost myself in God's presence. When I opened them, the steams of glory were all around me. It was like driving in the early morning fog. I could barely see the girl who was next to me. When I tried to ask her about it, my attention shifted to the natural realm, and the glory seemed to fade. In realizing this, I turned my affection back to worship as the cloud engulfed me again. I was in the middle of everyone, but it was like a separate world opened up around me... I guess I fell into a cosmic bubble.

A few years before I arrived at BRSM, there was a story of the glory appearing in one of Dr. Gladstone's classes as he taught about the glory of God filling Solomon's Temple. Suddenly, he heard gasps for air and the sounds of awe from his students. He looked up from his notes to see a that a cloud had formed in the middle of the auditorium. It was a greyish pillar that hovered in front of him. The rest of the school day became a first-hand lesson and encounter of God's glory as the students marinated in God's presence.

LAKE & WIGGLESWORTH

John G. Lake and Smith Wigglesworth are two of my favorite revivalists. The lives they lived were "otherworldly." They walked in unfathomable power for their generation, which inspiringly, is not that far away from our own.

Smith Wigglesworth was an Englishman who demonstrated unusual power throughout his ministry. One specific testimony that shocked me is the story of a man who that had no feet. Smith instructed the man to go to the shoe store. Unsurprisingly, the fellow did not think it was a good idea, but he went anyway. Upon arriving, the attendants said that they did not feel they could help him very much. In response, the man stated, "Well if I could wear shoes, what size do you think I would wear?" They looked him over for a moment and went and got a size they thought would fit him. They set the shoes in front of him, and the man stuck the nub of his leg down into the shoe. As he did, a brand-new foot grew out into the shoe! Next, he placed his other nub into the other shoe, and a new foot grew out into that shoe too! He stood up on his [new] feet, walked to the counter, paid for his shoes, and went on his way. Oh, my holy awesomeness! Yes, it happened! Our God is this radical.

LIGHTNINGS OF GOD

Now, we will zoom-in on John G. Lake and glean from the unique language he used to describe his heavenly encounters. In doing so, may we peer into his thought processes and learn to think like him. The goal is for us to capture and learn from Lake's mentality. The quotes I share with you to will give insight into the way he thought about, reacted to, and processed the Kingdom of God. All the quotes are from *John G. Lake; The Complete Collection of His Life's Teachings,* by Roberts Liardon.

> The lightnings of God went through me...[4]

"Lightnings" is how John G. Lake almost always described the power of God that lived in him, moved through him, and utterly possessed him.

> God Almighty can look out of your eyes, and every devil that was ever in hell could not look in the eyes of Jesus without crawling. The lightnings of God were there.[5]

He seemed to be on a different plane than most who lived in his day. He was on Earth, surrounded by Heaven. Lightning is energy in the sky connecting with energy on the Earth. What an excellent picture of the power of God that is available towards us who believe.

> I pray that the eyes of your heart may be enlightened, so that you will know what is the hope of His calling, what are the riches of the glory of His inheritance in the saints, and what is the surpassing greatness of His power toward us who believe. These are in accordance with the working of the strength of His might which He brought about in Christ, when He raised Him from the dead and seated Him at His right hand in the heavenly places, far above all rule and authority and power and dominion, and every name that is named, not only in this age but also in the one to come.
>
> Ephesians 1:18-21 NASB

And raised us up with Him, and seated us with Him in the heavenly places in Christ Jesus.

vv 2:6

THE TANGIBLE WORD

Lake was able to make such a statement because verses like these were not distant and far off. They were real, available, and tangible, written for him to walk in. He was not content to just read them. They were not fairy tales: They were realities. One of my dreams is to see a church that lives out the life described in the Bible—

TRANSLATING **HEAVENLY MYSTERIES** INTO **EARTHLY REALITIES.**

To live out the call in the Bible, and not merely theologize it away for a by-gone era, is a needed perspective in this hour. It's real, it's powerful, and it's for today! Salvation alone is an incomplete gospel. It is the first step in a transformed life. A life of fullness is one that is fully saved, fully healed, and fully delivered. It's a life restored to the image of God.

Lake described it this way:

> It is always God's will to heal... God is willing, just as willing to heal as He is to save. *Healing is part of salvation.* It is not separate from salvation. Healing was purchased by the blood of Jesus. This Book always connects salvation and healing.

We are instructed on the Word of God concerning the salvation of the soul, but our education concerning sickness and His desire and willingness to heal has been neglected. We have gone to the eighth grade or tenth grade or the University on the subject of salvation, but on the subject of healing we are in the ABC class. [6]

These statements were written on January 12, 1922! Lake was a man ahead of his time. In the areas of healing and supernatural activation, the church is just now catching up with a way-of-living Lake experienced almost a century ago.

I am part of a culture, which over the last 20 years, has envisioned Heaven coming to Earth as described in "The Lord's Prayer" (Matt 6:9-10):

Your Kingdom come...
Your will be done...
On Earth...
As it is in Heaven

The prayer is the key to a lifestyle of answered prayers as Heaven transforms the Earth through the ones who live out the prayer. Jesus brought the Kingdom of Heaven to the Earth, then passed it along to his disciples. Unfortunately, many in our generation misunderstand this and believe Jesus is throwing a "Hail Mary" pass to the "millennium." As a result, the cry for Heaven to come to Earth seems almost revolutionary for those whose goal in life is waiting for the "sweet bye and bye." Heaven is available here now, and Lake was tapping into these revelations years before the recent re-discovery.

THE BAPTISM OF THE HOLY GHOST

> A Christian is a man indwelt by God–the house of God, the tabernacle of the Most High! Man, indwelt by God, becomes the hands and the heart and the feet and the mind of Jesus Christ. God descends into man: man ascends into God! That is the purpose and the power of the baptism of the Holy Ghost.[7]

What theology! Have you ever heard it described in such a way? Most often it is lessened in its intensity. Therefore, the infilling of the Spirit in the individual seems to be lessened in its intensity as well. Even if you have been baptized in the Holy Spirit—immersed in the very flaming life of God Himself—there is still a greater baptism to undergo. We have access to the fullness of God, but God vastly out-stretches the universe.

Heavenly throne-room entities are always crying out in response to the more of God they see every time they behold Him, and they've been doing it for eons. They are front and center to the King of Majesty, yet still experience more. Their existence is a perpetual invitation for us to experience more of God every day we live, and in every breath we take. It is our access to His fullness that invites us into His more.

GOD IS A **LIVING LABYRINTH** FULL OF **WONDER** AND **INTRIGUE** WHO **INVITES US** TO **EXPLORE** THE **SECRETS ERUPTING** IN HIS **HEART.**

Lake understood the ascended lifestyle as the secret of seeing Heaven invade the Earth. Each ascent is another step in the building process. Each baptism dives deeper into the depths of God. As your mind reads, allow your spirit to listen as Lake describes his baptism in the Spirit:

> And one day, the glory of God in a new manifestation and a new incoming came to my life. And when the phenomena had passed, and the glory of it remained in my soul, I found that my life began to manifest in the varied range of the gifts of the Spirit, and I spoke in tongues by the power of God, and God flowed through me with a new force. Healings were of a more powerful order. Oh, God live in me, God manifested in me, God spoke through me. My spirit was deified, and I had a new comprehension of God's will, new discernment of spirit, new revelation of God in me.[8]

What strength, what substance, what description! He was changed and upgraded in this encounter. "Healings were of a more powerful order." Who talks like this today? We get excited about a healing if it happens at all, and that's a good thing. We need never to lose sight of such joys. But with Lake, we catch a glimpse into that which is found hidden within the ascent. Now we know that healings of a "more powerful order" are available and waiting for us.

Next, tells another experience in the Spirit, where he seemed to go deeper and experience more of God:

> In 1908, I preached at Pretoria, South Africa, when one-night God came over my life in such power, in such

streams of the liquid glory and power that it flowed consciously off my hands like streams of electricity.[9]

These encounters have created a description for him to articulate someone full of the Spirit:

> Will a man speak in tongues when he is baptized in the Holy Ghost? Yes, he will, and he will heal the sick when he is baptized, and he will glorify God out of the spirit of him with praises more delightful and heavenly than you ever heard. He will have a majestic bearing. He will look like the Lord Jesus Christ, and you will be like Him.[10]

"He will have a majestic bearing." An ascended lifestyle will speak in such a way that Heaven shines through our language.

THE POWER OF A CHRISTIAN

The same divine authority that was vested in Jesus is vested *by Jesus* in every Christian soul. Jesus made provision for the Church of Jesus Christ to go on forever and do the very same things He did and to keep doing them forever. That is what is the matter with the church. The church lost faith in that truth. The result was, they went on believing the He could save them from sin, but the other great range of the Christian life was left to the doctors and the devil or anything else. And the church will never be a real Church, in the real power of the living God again, until she comes back again to the original standard –where Jesus was.[11]

I confess I would like to swear sometimes, and I would like to say, "To h– with preachers who are all the time preaching fear." They preach fear of the devil and fear of demons and fear of this influence and fear of that influence and fear of some other power. If the Holy Ghost has come from heaven into your soul, common sense teaches us that He has made *you* the master thereby of every other power in the world.

Greater is He that is in you, than he that is in the world.

1 John 4:4

And if we had faith to believe that the 'greater then he' is in us, bless God, we would be stepping out with boldness and majesty. The conscious supremacy of the Son of God would be manifest in our lives and instead of being subservient and bowed down and broken beneath the weight of sin and the powers of darkness around us, *they* would flee from us and keep out of our way. I believe God there is not a devil that comes within a hundred feet of a real God-anointed Christian. That is the vision God put in my soul.[12]

He is a man who was not afraid of the enemy. He walked in boldness. Many in the church don't even mention the reality of demons and the powers of this age. The truth is that they do play a part in the Kingdom, which is total defeat. Lake sought to empower the Christian concerning

148

these matters by revealing that God has given us all the power and authority over these principalities.

> All these little insignificant devils that come along side in this sickness or that sickness or that temptation of sin have no power over you. Dear friends, from heaven there comes to your heart and mine that dominion of Jesus by which the God-anointed soul walks through them, through myriads of demons, and they cannot touch you.[13]

THE FIRE OF GOD

I want to leave you with a story that Lake shares of how the fire spread in South Africa through a man named Don VanVuuren. He was sick with tuberculosis, so his friends sent him a letter telling him of how God was moving among them through Lake's ministry. As he read the letter he was deeply moved and cried out to God to be made whole. Within a few minutes, he could breathe deeply. He experienced complete healing and the baptism of the Spirit, all from reading the letter. His wife, who wanted nothing to do with God, saw the change in her husband and the healing of his body. She gave her life to Jesus right then. Within a week, their whole household of 13 people were all saved and filled with the Spirit. The fire spread to the community, baptizing another 19 families in the Holy Spirit.

Soon after the flames began to burn in VanVuuren, God told him to go to Pretoria and speak to parliament. Upon arriving, he gained admittance with Premier Botha, who tells of their meeting:

...that man came into my office and stood ten feet from my desk. I looked up, and before he commenced to speak, I began to shake and rattle in my chair. I knelt down. I had to put my head under the desk and cry to God, why he looked like God, he talked like God. [Lake adds] he had the majesty of God. He was super-humanly wonderful.

For 18 days he went to different leaders of the government "until every high official knew there was a God and a Christ and a Savior and a Baptism of the Holy Spirit."

For several years before I left Africa, VanVuuren went up and down the land like a burning fire. Everywhere he went sinners were saved and were healed. Men and women were baptized in the Holy Ghost, until he set the districts on fire with the power of God... [14]

May the life of John G. Lake inspire you to become living and breathing transmitter of heaven. I believe that if our minds can intercept the transformational thinking he tapped into, we will see the power of God, like never before.

WILL YOU BECOME A REVIVALIST?

It is my heart that this brief overview of testimonies from early revivals and revivalists, along with the glimpse into the lives of Lake and Wigglesworth have stirred you to become a revivalist. Did you begin to burn and the stories of the supernatural? Do you long to walk in more power than you have yet to experience? Today could be the day someone says to you, "I think you have the power."

ACTIVATION

There is always more of God to experience. Whether you have been filled with the Holy Spirit once, many times, or have yet to experience this glorious encounter, today is the day for more. Ask God to fill you with His Spirit. Write out what you experience below:

DECLARATION

I set my heart to being a revivalist. I am a revivalist. I will answer the call of a revivalist. Lord, make me a revivalist. I long to show to the world the supernatural power of God. Demonstrate Yourself in my life, God, that those around me may know that you are Lord. In Jesus Name!

RISE REVIVALISTS!

NOTES

[1] Roberts Lairdon, *God's Generals; Why They Succeeded; Why Some failed* (Tulsa, Albury, 1996). p 112.

[2] ibid, p. 81.

[3] The Sentinel Group, The Hebrides Revival: A Retrospective (2007), http://www.sentinelgroup.org/the-hebrides-revival.html: http://www.sentinelgroup.org (2018). Other revival materials, including the Transformation DVD's, are available on the Sentinel Group website: sentinelgroup.org (2018). The Sentinel Group now offers Journey to Transformation (JTT) courses – a distillation of what they have learned from hundreds of contemporary and historical cases of transforming revival: http://www.sentinelgroup.org/jtt.html (2018). Used with permission.

[4] Roberts Liardon, *John G. Lake; The Complete Collection of His Life Teachings,* (Tulsa, Albury Publishing 1999), p. 447.

[5] Ibid

[6] Ibid. p. 407.

[7] Ibid. p. 367.

[8] Ibid. p. 372

[9] ibid, p. 376-377.

[10] Ibid. p. 378.

[11] Ibid. p. 411-412.

[12] Ibid. p. 442.

[13] Ibid. p. 448.

[14] Ibid. p. 456-451; p. 457; p. 459. This entire section contains contextual paraphrasing the story of VanVuuren.

SEVEN

SIGNS OF THE KINGDOM

**THE CENTER OF THE KINGDOM IS
WHEREVER THE KING ABIDES.**

Heaven. Where is it? What is it? What is the Kingdom of Heaven? Much has been written, discussed, and considered as potential answers to these questions throughout the ages. We could revisit famous answers from the renown. We could dissect the original languages to broaden the scope. We could perform an endless array of methods and still end up where we started at the beginning of this paragraph.

All aspects of the Kingdom are in relation to the King. Only through the King is the King's Domain understood. Many have tried to find the definition by surveying the lands of the King without actually knowing the King Himself. The center of the Kingdom isn't a geographical location somewhere in the space or the middle of the universe. The center of the Kingdom is wherever the King is—wherever He happens to be at the moment. Yes, He is everywhere, but where is His Majesty welcome and on display?

Jesus is the King of Kings, the pinnacle of everything, and the Source of everything known and unknown. The mysteries of the Kingdom of Heaven are hidden in Him, only discoverable through relationship, intimacy, and a life spent in His presence. If we attempt to answer these questions outside of Him, we may come up with good ideas, but they will not be perfect. He is the culmination of all things. If we make the ministry to Jesus our chief assignment in life, everything else will be added.

THE LORD'S PRAYER

I have introduced and expanded upon The Lord's prayer a couple of times already, so here, we are going to zoom out and take a wider view. I want to consider the prayer as a whole and the implications of such a perspective.

A LIFE LIVED IN THE PRESENCE OF THE KING WILL BE ONE THAT IS EMPOWERED TO DISPLAY AND EXERCISE THE KING'S DOMINION.

It is the desire of the King for everyone in His Kingdom to discover their unique destiny and identity in Him. When King Jesus walked the Earth, He demonstrated the lifestyle of the Kingdom, revealing His profound relationship with His Father. Jesus would often demonstrate first and give instruction after. When Jesus taught his disciples how to pray, it was the key to activating a Kingdom lifestyle. His teachings are a construct of Heaven on Earth.

The Lord's Prayer is one of the most powerful, cosmic, and heavenly passages in literature. It's popular and well known, even prayed by millions daily. Sadly, the enormity of revelation and wonders it contains is easily bypassed via rapid repetition by those desperately trying to please a God they barely know. Prayer, in general, is often seen as sending a request form up to the boss with little hope left for a response. The Lord's Prayer is no different. Prayer viewed through the lenses of formulating words to warrant a response from God misses the entire point of "praying." This modus operandi is how the church has primarily prayed this passage for the last 2000 years.

Fortunately, if you have been involved in Kingdom culture, these verses have become a lifestyle. Before Jesus shares the prayer, He states that endlessly repeating it is pointless (vv 7-8). There is nothing wrong with praying the prayer itself if you capture the essence of what Jesus intends. The secrets revealed in this prayer are designed to shape our prayer-life. It aligns us with Heaven, making us able to reveal Heaven on Earth, just like Jesus. As we examine the prayer, a whole new world will open up before us. It's so much more than a few lines to memorize; it's an open door into the way the heart of the Son moves the heart of the Father. This prayer is our invitation to such a relationship.

> Pray, then, in this way: 'Our Father who is in heaven, hallowed be Your name. 'Your kingdom come. Your will be done, on earth as it is in heaven. 'Give us this day our daily bread. 'And forgive us our debts, as we also have forgiven our debtors. 'And do not lead us into

temptation, but deliver us from evil. [For Yours is the kingdom and the power and the glory forever. Amen.']

Matthew 6:9-13 NASB

Jesus proves that prayer is so much more than petitions. It even goes beyond conversation. It is a way of being. He begins by revealing Heaven's agenda to fill the Earth. He instructs "us" to pray like this. Therefore, "we" pray to our Father in Heaven—whose name is "hallowed" or "set apart"-"other than" the world.

To "Him who is set apart," we pray "Your Kingdom Come!" Likewise, "Your Will be Done! The Father's will is for His Kingdom to go and respond to those on the Earth who have summoned. He plans to give all of the Earth all of Heaven. Jesus understood this and lived it out. Now He shows His disciples—even us—the will and desire of His Father. This desire is the design of all creation. His "will" is and is becoming the will of this world. His Kingdom is and is becoming the Kingdom of this world.

"On Earth as in Heaven" is the goal. Through the advancement of the Kingdom, His will fills the Earth—transforming and recreating it to the "kind intention of his will," (Eph 1:5). "Will" resides within us. When His "will" becomes my will, then my mind has been transformed (Romans 12:1-2) into His mind (1 Cor 2:16). This transformed way of thinking becomes the director of my prayers. When I pray, it is always with this in mind: His Kingdom comes, and His will is done through me.

THE MINISTRY OF JESUS

If Jesus said that praying this way invites His Father's Kingdom to come, then His life is probably a pretty good picture of what this looks like. Most of us, whether believers or not, know the stories: He turned water into wine, walked on water, healed the sick, raised the dead, cleansed lepers, overcame the devil, raised up disciples, opened up Heaven on Earth on the Mt. of Transfiguration, and did good to all. I could go on and on.

> Now there are also many other things that Jesus did. Were every one of them to be written, I suppose that the world itself could not contain the books that would be written.
>
> John 21:25 ESV

The issue of supernatural ministry is essentially the fundamental issue of the ministry of Jesus. Not only did His ministerial approach found the church, but is also the way He builds the church today and expands His Kingdom. If we are truly Christians, then His ministry will be present within us. If the genuine ministry of Jesus is present, then signs, wonders, and miracles will also be present. These characteristics encapsulate His ministry and will be present in the ministries who claim to function in His name, lest they fall short of His method.

LIMITLESS LOVE

> For I am sure that neither death nor life, nor angels nor rulers, nor things present nor things to come, nor

157

powers, nor height nor depth, nor anything else in all creation, will be able to separate us from the love of God in Christ Jesus our Lord.

Jesus restores a relationship with His Father to creation through loving without an agenda.

HIS LIMITLESS LOVE ERASES SIN, ERADICATES DISEASE, EVICTS DEATH, AND UNLOCKS DESTINY.

No sickness, poverty, abuse, natural boundaries, violence, nor whatever else could stop His love. If a mountain stands in the way of love, then the mountain must forfeit its terrain. If gravity, then gravity: If oxygen, then oxygen, if "____," then "¬-____." It doesn't matter what fills in the blank; His love is unstoppable, revealed through those who love for the sake of the One who is Love.

The world has a mask blocking it from the true supernatural power embedded in creation for it to experience. This prayer is a revolution that reveals that Father God is the power behind everything, and is the secret plan of Heaven's invasion of Earth through us. His story continues and expands in us. To say that He removed the supernatural ministry of Holy Spirit after the establishment of the church is also to say that He removed His ministry from the Earth. If this is true, then there is no need for a church. As Dr. Gladstone says, "A church that is not clothed in supernatural power is naked and undesirable." Jesus desires a church that is His body, which is only fully alive when they do what He did in greater magnitude. If His body believes that they are not supernatural,

158

they are either serving another "jesus," or they critically lack the fullness of Christ and the likeness of His image.

The Lord's Prayer is a gateway for us to discover who are true supernatural inheritance in Him. It is an invitation into that which is greater in the Christian existence. Experience His limitless love in limitless ways. The table is set for you to dine on His fullness and become everything He created you to be. It is a family prayer.

REVEALERS OF THE KINGDOM

In fulfilling the Old Covenant, Jesus inaugurated the New Covenant. In the Old, the Kingdom was progressively revealed over thousands of years. The generation alive when Jesus lived in Israel had an atmosphere of expectation for the coming Messiah. Much of their understanding of the Kingdom was naturally exclusive. They expected a Messiah that would restore the earthly Kingdom of Israel. The Messiah who came was supernaturally inclusive. He restored the Kingdom of Heaven to all creation.

One of the first declarations Jesus made was "repent, for the Kingdom of Heaven is at hand." This statement declared to the Earth that the Kingdom, which was always coming, has arrived. As we established earlier, the Kingdom is wherever the King is. Fellowship with the King transforms us into ambassadors of the Kingdom. If He resides in us, then His Kingdom resides in us. If his Kingdom expands through us, then it will expand in the same manner it expanded through the King Himself. He is the model of ministry—the administration of the Kingdom. The ekklesia—church—is His body of government. As the church, we establish and govern Heaven on Earth. The realization of the King's design can only occur if the church reveals the Kingdom with the same supernatural demonstration of God's love as Jesus did.

Jesus set us up to "outdo" Him. Like David giving Solomon everything He needed to build the temple, Jesus ascended and sent us Spirit, giving us everything we need to build.

> Truly, truly, I say to you, whoever believes in me will also do the works that I do; and greater works than these will he do, because I am going to the Father.
>
> John 14:12 ESV

Heaven longs to fill the earth. Creation groans to receive a baptism of supernatural love. Jesus has equipped us to meet this need with His precious Holy Spirit. His plan all along was to "clone" Himself in us.

JESUS MAKES US POWERFUL ENOUGH TO LOVE THE SIN OUT OF SOMEONE, TO HEAL THE SICKNESS OUT SOMEONE, AND TO CAST THE DEVIL OUT OF SOMEONE.

"Here I am," screams the creation. "Here we are" shouts the galaxies. Face in the wind, and we must see to believe? The secret is that when we believe they will see. Our perspective should be the most hope-filled in the universe.

WE HAVE THE ANSWER TO EVERY QUESTION—JESUS.

While writing this chapter as I sat in a coffee shop, I heard a man say, "Sooner or later the weather's gonna get better; it's got to." I thought he

160

said, "Sooner, or later the world's gonna get better, it's got to." He left with a smile on his face as he looked out the window at a rainy, cold, overcast day. This man captured the sunshine in the midst of the rain.

OUR **BELIEF SYSTEMS** NEED A **LIFE SHIFT.**

Even natural elements cause those without hope to be afraid. The focus of the church since the World Wars has darkened and twisted into a victimized belief system, hoping Jesus will rescue them from the storm of the times. The peace in us is greater than any storm. Storms are incapable of sinking the Jesus who lives in us. Why would we preach death when the Author of Life lives inside us? We must stop being death to the world; we must become life. If Jesus came to give life, then we must give life.

THEOLOGY AND MYSTERION

The study and discussion of the Bible are important and vital to our lives—*Theology*. However, this is only one side of the coin. It is just as important to experience the Word—*Mysterion*. It is one thing *to know* all about the Bible—the Word of God—but it is another thing to encounter it. If we preach a message we have not experienced, then our testimony is either invalid or severely incomplete. To know it and memorize it is essential, but it's not the end. Beyond knowing the Word, we must become it.

The sons of Sceva found this out the hard way. They knew the message, and they knew the messenger, Paul, but they didn't know Jesus Himself. They heard something they had yet to become. The listened to a theory they did not digest. Their head knowledge had not traveled to

161

their hearts. Therefore, they had no history with Jesus—no supernatural substance to meet the need of the situation before them.

> And God was doing extraordinary miracles by the hands of Paul, so that even handkerchiefs or aprons that had touched his skin were carried away to the sick, and their diseases left them and the evil spirits came out of them. Then some of the itinerant Jewish exorcists undertook to invoke the name of the Lord Jesus over those who had evil spirits, saying, "I adjure you by the Jesus whom Paul proclaims." Seven sons of a Jewish high priest named Sceva were doing this. But the evil spirit answered them, "Jesus I know, and Paul I recognize, but who are you?" And the man in whom was the evil spirit leaped on them, mastered all of them and overpowered them, so that they fled out of that house naked and wounded. And this became known to all the residents of Ephesus, both Jews and Greeks. And fear fell upon them all, and the name of the Lord Jesus was extolled.

> Acts 19:11-17 ESV

As this passage clearly details, the devil is not threatened by a powerless theology. Only when we experience the Kingdom of Heaven through our relationship with Jesus will we have any impact on the supernatural realm. Supernatural power begins by believing in a supernatural Gospel. A non-supernatural Gospel is not good news, its inferior news. A "knowledge only" Gospel is a powerless one. The location of true knowledge is in the experience. When you experience God, then the mystery of who He is in you is discovered. This discovery breeds the wisdom of Heaven bred in supernatural witness. Yes, many scholars argue that the sons of Sceva had only selfish motives, but what if that is a surface level observation? Maybe they were inspired by Paul and the demonstration of the Kingdom in their midst. Whatever their agenda was, it contained knowledge without power.

> But realize this, that in the last days difficult times will come. For men will be lovers of self, lovers of money, boastful, arrogant, revilers, disobedient to parents, ungrateful, unholy, unloving, irreconcilable, malicious gossips, without self-control, brutal, haters of good, treacherous, reckless, conceited, lovers of pleasure rather than lovers of God, holding

> to a form of godliness, although they have denied its power; Avoid such men as these.

> 2 Timothy 3:1-5 ESV

This passage places those who deny the power of God in the same category as the boastful, arrogant, and unholy. Transformed lives are a manifestation of the power of God. You can read the Word until you're blue in the face, but you'll never change until you experience it.

In the ministry of Jesus, creation recognized the difference between those who talked about theology, and that of a Son, who was able to demonstrate the mystery.

And they were astonished at his teaching, for he taught them as one who had authority, and not as the scribes.

Mark 1:22 ESV

We could all study the Word more, but let our intention be to experience the relationship with God the Bible invites us to experience.

WISDOM IS KNOWLEDGE EXPERIENCED.

The Bible points our individually unknown journeys toward a relationship with God. Mysterion is the discovery of hidden treasures. In searching them out, we encounter more of who God is.

THE WATCHDOG SOCIETIES

Most of the time, the people Jesus rebuked where those who denied supernatural power. Today we have whole "Watchdog Societies" whose goal is to "watch out for," and to track down and attack individuals and ministries who display the supernatural power of God. Sadly, their "ministry" is to tear apart those different than their own. For many, verses warning against deception are used out of context to support their powerless worldviews. I mentioned earlier that when Jesus walked the Earth, many missed His appearing because they had a natural view of the fulfillment of the Kingdom, rather than a supernatural one. This same perspective continues today. It's theology without mysterion. They feel that those experiencing signs and wonders are deceived, and preach to those who will listen that the devil is the one who empowers the wonderworkers.

And the scribes who came down from Jerusalem were saying, "He is possessed by Beelzebul," and "by the prince of demons he casts out the demons." And he called them to him and said to them in parables, "How can Satan cast out Satan? If a kingdom is divided against itself, that kingdom cannot stand. And if a house is divided against itself, that house will not be able to stand. And if Satan has risen up against himself and is divided, he cannot stand, but is coming to an end. But no one can enter a strong man's house and plunder his goods, unless he first binds the strong man. Then indeed he may plunder his house.

Truly, I say to you, all sins will be forgiven the children of man, and whatever blasphemies they utter, but whoever blasphemes against the Holy Spirit never has forgiveness, but is guilty of an eternal sin"— for they were saying, "He has an unclean spirit.

Mark 3:22-30 ESV

This key section of Scripture makes us aware of the enemy's schemes when accusing those who demonstrate the power of the Spirit. Satan's tactic is to attribute the miracles of the Holy Spirit to demons.

Without a supernatural worldview, fear can misdiagnose the experience of the supernatural realm. This reaction falsifies the encounter's in the mind, causing it to believe all supernatural experiences as evil, new age, or from sources other than God.

Jesus exposes the deception by revealing that not even Satan would fight against his own house. Satan was upset that the demon was cast out, and, in an effort to cease the supernatural activity of Jesus, he attempted to deceive the religious leaders and the people into thinking that this was a demonic phenomenon.

Jesus goes on to say that if one operates under the guise of this deception, it is blasphemy of the Holy Spirit. Blasphemy is an irreverence for the holy or otherworldly. It also claims the attributes of the divine. Jesus is jealous to protect the ministry of the Holy Spirit and goes as far to say that if you blaspheme Holy Spirit, it will never be forgiven.

When he made this statement, he didn't condemn everyone present. He didn't' even condemn those making the statements. Rather, it was a clarion warning for those listening, and for all of those who would find themselves at a similar crossroads. Do not attribute the acts of the Holy Spirit to demons. Confusion on this can lead to deception, which can lead to a warped reality of who God really is. This downward spiral can produce a state of thinking where one actually knows the work of the Spirit and seeks to deceive people into believing that these works are demonic. The end result is that they have now blasphemed Holy Spirit.

This story contains a stern warning that is placed there for our protection and discernment. It is one of the many bumpers Jesus has placed in our lives to ensure we keep bowling strikes with our destinies. With this in mind, if you find yourself in a similar situation, you will know the nature of Heaven, and be able to clearly identify the source of the situation. It is not a license to accuse people of blasphemy, rather it is a chance to throw out a life vest, and gently pull them back to safety.

The ministry of Jesus was entirely supernatural. It is evident in His private ministry to the Father and His public ministry to the people. The ones who teach that there is no supernatural power sound more like the ones Jesus preached against, and the ones who walk in power look more like the disciples. So if you get rebuked for seeking signs and wonders, you're in good company. The Pharisees and Sadducees knew the Word more than any other in their time, but they missed the season of power and visitation. How could this be? It's hard to believe, but this is precisely what these groups are doing today.

God continues to move in wonderful supernatural ways from generation to generation. Every time He does something new, it is common for the "old guard" to misunderstand it. Often, this happens because the new generation that steps out and receives the new move of God responds like a child getting a new toy. If I give a child a bike, he needs to learn how to ride it before he enters a race. It is the same with the gifts of God. We grow in the gift as we develop in our relationship with God. As this growth occurs, mistakes will be made because we are learning. If a child learns to ride a bike, he will likely fall many times before he masters his balance. However, it would be ridiculous for me to accuse him of not riding a "real bike" just because he is shaky, sometimes falls, and hasn't quite figured it out yet.

This illustration provides an example of how people label those who are experiencing new supernatural movements as "strange fire," false, whacky, fleshly, demonic, etc. Is everyone perfect? No. Do some people report strange encounters? Yes. Do they say things that seem contrary to Scripture? Absolutely. Are they perfect? No. I ask you again, are they perfect? And again you respond with a resounding "NO!" So is it ok for them to mess up? Most would say yes, when in their hearts, the answer is no. What if someone is caught in adultery? How would Jesus treat them?

> And as they continued to ask him, he stood up and said to them, "Let him who is without sin among you be the first to throw a stone at her.

John 8:7 ESV

Someone who messes-up within the realms of the supernatural is unforgivable to most of these "Watchdog Societies," yet the ones who accuse are not perfect themselves. Let me ask you this: Who looks more like Moses, the prophets, Jesus, the apostles and those in the early church? What if we look throughout church history? Is it the one with supernatural testimonies or the one who accuses? Compare their lives to the Bible and tell me who looks more Christ-like? It is those who embrace the supernatural lifestyle. They push beyond the limits of "logic and reason" into the mysterious "depths of God."

THESE SIGNS

What does the Kingdom look like on the Earth? Jesus explains:

> And these signs will accompany those who believe: in my name they will cast out demons; they will speak in new tongues; they will pick up serpents with their hands; and if they drink any deadly poison, it will not hurt them; they will lay their hands on the sick, and they will recover.

Mark 16:17-18 ESV

Most of the ones who take a stand against the supernatural do not heal the sick, raise the dead, cast out demons, cleanse lepers, prophesy, speak in tongues, interpret tongues, have faith, see miracles, signs, and wonders, or operate in words of wisdom and knowledge. The stories of the ones who lived in the times archived in the Bible for our benefit to inspire us to write new supernatural tales in our generation. Which life more fulfills the Word, the one that talks about it, or the one that becomes it? Which one becomes a written testimony of Jesus? Who are the real apostles—the ones "sent" of God to change a culture to that of Heaven?

> The signs of a true apostle were performed among you with all perseverance, by signs and wonders and miracles.

> 2 Corinthians 12:12 NASB

"Signs" and "Wonders" and "Miracles," are the things I hear people rebuke Kingdom theology for the most when they are the only criteria Paul uses to defend his apostleship.

My heart is to see the church ignited in the supernatural power Jesus paid the price to deliver to her through sending His Spirit to fill her and guide her into her destiny. This hour is the time given to us out of all the other generations. Let's make the most of it! We have the good news of an awesome Jesus, who is King of an awesome Kingdom, in-which reside an awesome people. His "awesomeness" is unlimited and peppered throughout all creation.

JESUS INVITES **YOU** TO **EXPERIENCE HIM** IN EVEN **GREATER,** MORE **UNFATHOMABLE WAYS.**

You don't have to be afraid of "strange fire" in the pursuit of the supernatural power of God. His true Fire always burns up the strange fire. The enemy is afraid of the power of God and does anything he can to stop it from spreading and setting the church on fire.

A CHURCH ON FIRE WILL SET THE **WORLD ON FIRE** AND **RAZE** THE **DEVIL'S** REMAINING **STRONGHOLDS** IN THE **PROCESS.**

We live in an age where everyone can sit behind a computer screen and share their thoughts on the internet. Having access to the web doesn't make you an expert. Many watchdogs project their micro worldview on everything that is different. They "troll" men and women of power with accusations and constant slander. Such malice is not the Spirit of Jesus.

Many of them do love God, but have a warped view of His goodness, believing that crushing their brothers and sisters pleases Him. Others have been hurt by the church, experienced rejection, or in a twisted reality, hope to find recognition from the ones they are denouncing.

I pray that the watchdogs have radical encounters and discover the true nature of Jesus. I pray His love transforms their hearts, so they can see how good He is and how loved they are. When we know who God is, and know who we are, we will see how lovely He made everyone around us to be.

Jesus is King, and He is roaring like a Lion. It does not say "Behold the Kitty Cat." He is not the Kitty Cat of Judah: He is the Lion of Judah. He is the Lion who devours sickness. The very reason He ascended was so He could send us His Spirit, to ignite in us a supernatural lifestyle. To say that God took His power back seventy-five years later is to say that He said, the "church and the Bible are enough; I can get off my throne now." The apex of his time on Earth was not the cross; it was the ascension. What is the cross without the resurrection and the ascension? He said what He did was not complete until He ascended. He intended to make us like Him, to make us lions. We are lions, not kitty cats. We need to remove ourselves from kitty cat Christianity. The world doesn't need kitty cats that snuggle up next to their diseases and problems. They need lions who come in the power of the Kingdom of Heaven and unleash the Father's heart on them in the form of Holy Spirit power!

What is the Kingdom? It is the answer to any need creation may have through the demonstration of the power, love, and wisdom of Jesus Christ present within a people who are known by His name. "Any need" even includes dismantling death with the power of resurrection, as we will discover in the next chapter.

"Heaven on Earth," "Kingdom," "Ascension," "Supernatural Lifestyle," "Power," "Signs, Wonders, and Miracles," are key themes you have read multiple times up to this point in the book. As a fitness coach, I train clients through repetition to build muscle, develop motor memory, and burn calories. Revivalists are "FIT" for the Kingdom. Repetition rewires thought patterns in the brain. The more you read it, the more you will become it. Then you'll be able to reproduce it without thinking because it has become part of your nature. When I mention "Kingdom," it is like doing another rep. Your apprehension of it expands each time.

ACTIVATION

Pray this with me, "Lord, make me a Lion. Forgive me for living like a kitty cat when you have destined me to be so much more. Teach me how to roar!" We are not kitties... We are not furry little fluffies... We are Lions... "Make me a lion, Lord!"

1. How can I spend more time in the secret place?

2. What is one way I can reveal Heaven on Earth today?

DECLARATION

I will be a carrier of the Kingdom. I will see your miraculous power. I am a lion. I am a revivalist. Lord, raise me up in the Heavenly Family to be equipped in Your ways, that I may look just like you to the nation.

RISE REVIVALISTS!

EIGHT

VOICE OF RESURRECTION

THE QUEST OF HUANITY IS FREEDOM FROM THE POWER OF DEATH.

The hope to live beyond death is the assurance of the Christian and the secret escape for the atheist. Deep down, no one wants to die. Life is the foundation of creation. Death wasn't present until a lower form of living was introduced. Since then, mankind has sought after every possible method to avoid death, even at the cost of world war. On the positive side, much of humanity's greatest scientific breakthroughs have been in effort to solve the riddle of death.

The church has responded to the complexity of death, healing, and life in often conflicting ways. One view is that doctors are the only way God heals today, unless, by His sovereignty, He chooses to heal someone Himself. The other view is that doctors are of the devil. The first view misses the reality that God desires to heal all. The second view misses the fact that doctors are good and help many people recover.

NATURAL AND DIVINE HEALING

I believe in doctors and medicine, and that they are gifts from God designed for us to live long, healthy lives. Each generation lives longer as humanity discovers new truths. Bill Johnson says, "There are things that are true and things that are truer." Justin Abraham expands, "There are truths, then there are higher truths." Both elements may be true. One truth may be the prototype, while the other is the archetype. One truth expands into the greater truth. Healing through medicine is true and good. Yet, there is a higher truth, healing through the Holy Spirit. What if they were never meant to be separate? The Creator gives us everything we need to sustain and nourish our earthly bodies. Also, our bodies are set within our spirits, providing intelligence and spiritual energy to our natural animation. Higher truth reveals that we reside in the presence of God. He is the Source of all life. Natural healing may come through doctors, supernatural healing, or divine realization of His thoughts towards us. He sees us as whole. When we think this way about ourselves, we align with His divine wholeness.

HIS PRESENCE IS AN ATMOSPHERE
DEATH CANNOT SURVIVE IN.

All three levels of truth are true, and God-given. We have full access to them all, yet we may rely on lower truths and neglect the higher truth that as God kids, He created us to live with Him forever.

Physicians reflect The Great Physician. I believe God heals supernaturally. If sickness comes my way, or if I hear of it affecting someone, my first response is always that God heals. While this truth is the cornerstone of my belief system, I will still utilize all the truths given to me. If I need a doctor or medicine, I will pull on those God-given resources in my life. This response doesn't cancel-out the great truth—divine healing—nor does it mean I lack faith. On the contrary, it takes faith for me to see a doctor. As I thank God for natural healers and healing methods, I know that I am supernatural and that His plan for me, my family, my friends, and everyone else is immediate, total, and perfect healing.

The Earth is full answers that reflect His nature and goodness. A Supernatural worldview has eyes to see these mysteries hidden in plain sight. When His earthly goodness is supercharged by His heavenly goodness, we discover the kind intention of His will, that which is good, acceptable, and perfect (Romans 12:2). We understand the truths available to us in natural healing, and that even if it's natural, it can also be supernatural because it too is a gift from God. As we proceed, we will focus on the divine while not forsaking other truths.

RESURRECTION LIFESTYLE

Resurrection is an essential element of the Kingdom. Jesus rose from the dead, giving life to all who believe in Him. His ascension gives believers the power to raise the dead.

A **RESURRECTION LIFESTYLE** IS THE **ATMOSPHERE** OF THE **BELIEVER**.

175

It is the framework of who we are. Death is unanswerable apart from the One who gives life. And if the One who gives life resides in us, then we have the answer the world is in search of.

The belief in resurrection sets us apart from other belief systems. The idea that everyone who has died will one day rise again seems impossible. The idea that a human can speak to a dead body and command life to return seems even more outrageous. Skipping death altogether sounds looney. However, there are those who have.

As Christians, resurrection is central to what we believe. The resurrection of Jesus is the key to our theology and entrance into eternal bliss. Belief in resurrection shocks the world.

> But perceiving that one group were Sadducees and the other Pharisees, Paul began crying out in the Council, "Brethren, I am a Pharisee, a son of Pharisees; I am on trial for the hope and resurrection of the dead!
>
> Acts 23:6 NASB
>
> Other than for this one statement which I shouted out while standing among them, 'For the resurrection of the dead I am on trial before you today.
>
> (vv 24:21)

According to these texts, the primary reason Paul was put on trial is that he preached the resurrection of the dead.

What kind of person can make such a report or share such good news as this? It is like saying:

I have the answer the world longs to hear. You no longer
have to worry about death. A man called Jesus overcame
death. He ascended to Heaven and is sitting at the right
hand of God. So, if you believe in Him, you will not have
to face death, but there is eternal life through him!

There can only be two responses to this: 1) Life invades the hearts of those who hear it; 2) Death rages against it. Justin Abraham reveals how the influence of death over the mind of many Christians causes them to misunderstand God and their access to Heaven in his simple, perspective-shattering statement, "Death isn't the savior, Jesus is." Unconsciously, many believers feel that it is only through death that they will enter eternal life, see the Kingdom, or experience Heaven. Jesus has already paid the price of death, giving us the joy of experiencing all of these things now. When this becomes our lifestyle, we reveal Heaven on the Earth. His death is our life. We are the answer to the problem of death when His life is resurgent in us, empowering us to awaken those captured by death's slumber.

LAZARUS

Jesus's friend Lazarus had fallen asleep and died. Lazarus' friends and family sent word when he was still alive that he was sick, asking Jesus to come. Jesus waited a couple of days, then made the journey. When He arrived, they were upset and said, "only if you had been here, Lazarus would not have died," (John 11:21).

Jesus said to her, 'I am the resurrection and the life; he
who believes in me will live, even if he dies, and everyone

who lives and believes in Me will never die, Do you believe this?'

John 11:25-26 NASB

They believed in the resurrection of the dead, but thought it was some distant promise reserved for a future age, not realizing the Resurrection Himself was standing face-to-face with them. Resurrection was an idea, a theology they believed in, not ascertaining that the idea was a living Person. They trusted Jesus with the truth of divine healing, but He was there to introduce them to a higher truth, resurrection.

Even though they didn't know what was happening, they believed in Jesus and brought Him to Lazarus' tomb when He asked. They trusted Him, even in disappointment, giving them access to the next encounter. It stretched their faith to do so, but their love for Jesus outweighed their objections. Jesus was about to reveal that he was more than their previous experience and relationship with Him had proved, as they would soon experience the magnitude of his power.

Jesus said, 'Remove the stone.' Martha, the sister of the deceased, said to Him, 'Lord, by this time there will be a stench, for he has been dead four days.' Jesus said to her, 'Did I not say to you that if you believe, you will see the glory of God?' So they removed the stone Then Jesus raised His eyes, and said, 'Father, I thank You that You have heard Me. I knew that You always hear Me; but because of the people standing around I said it, so that they may believe that You sent Me.' When He had said these things, He cried out with a loud voice,

'Lazarus, come forth.' The man who had died came forth, bound hand and foot with wrappings, and his face was wrapped around with a cloth. Jesus said to them, 'Unbind him, and let him go.' Therefore, many of the Jews who came to Mary, and saw what He had done, believed in Him.

John 11:39-44 NASB

HIS VOICE BREAKS THE BARRIER

Jesus did not just speak into Lazarus' tomb, nor did He merely speak to those who could hear. His voice broke the barrier! The sound waves traveled beyond the borders the natural realm. He spoke into death and called Lazarus back to life. He smashed death. He eradicated its powers, rendering it useless, null and void. He cleared the airways of unbelief and manifested the Kingdom in their midst. His voice of resurrection revealed Him as the architect of life, time, and space. He was a man who could speak in such a way that eternity had to respond to His command.

Interestingly, Jesus only spoke to benefit those proximate to Him. He walked in a constant awareness that His Father always heard Him. Therefore, He spoke to activate their faith, making a connection between the Voice they heard and the miracle they witnessed. This speech wasn't a singular event. It was a revealing of His Voice and the power it commands for the generations to come. Declaring His name in the Earth makes us as powerful as He, which is why He gave us His name to speak. His name grants us the same relationship with the Father He has. This connection is broadcast when we speak the name of Jesus into any event or circumstance.

Jesus wasn't challenged in raising Lazarus from the dead. He was challenged in ONLY raising Lazarus from the dead. If he had only said "Come forth!", then the entirety of those who had passed away from the beginning of time until then would have risen.

The value of His Voice in our lives is precious. Remember, it is only realized through relationship. When we speak His name, we recite the anthem of our hearts. We must be careful, as we saw with the Sons of Sceva, not to try and clone someone else's relationship with Jesus, and produce power without a relationship. Even if God honored our request, we would still miss the most important thing. Time with Jesus is revealed in opportunities to declare His name. Jesus could declare life to Lazarus because of his proximity to his Father.

AS **JESUS SPOKE**, THE **VOLUME** OF **HIS HISTORY** WITH **FATHER**, BOTH ON THE **EARTH**, AND FOR **EONS PASSED**, WAS **RELEASED** INTO **CREATION**.

There was no way Lazarus could've remained dead. The Author of Life and Creator of all summoned Him from death into life. Lazarus' resurrection was a moment for the ages. It was a baptism into the realm of the impossible for those who witnessed such majesty. "Shock and awe" filled the landscape as that which was unthinkable manifested before them. Not even death could stop Jesus. This raised the bar for His disciples. He had demonstrated the magnitude of power he was commissioning them to walk in.

Heal the sick, raise the dead, cleanse those who have leprosy, drive out demons. Freely you have received, freely give."

Matthew 10:8 NASB

ASCENSION THEOLOGY

The commission to the disciples was not a one-generation calling. It is the same commission before us today. We read the stories of Jesus to equip and activate us to walk in the power of Jesus.

Jesus is no longer on the Earth physically. But, as John 14-18 states, He did not leave us alone. He sent Holy Spirit to live in us. And through Holy Spirit, nothing—NO THING—is impossible.

My wife has a bracelet that says "Make the Impossible Possible." She wears it everywhere she goes. It is a constant declaration of the God that can do anything, lives inside her, ready to use her to do the impossible.

Jesus is the Sacrifice, the Resurrection, and the Ascension! It is significant and vital for us to understand all three. The cross, impressive as it is, is useless without the resurrection and ascension. Yes, the cross is the payment of our sins, but without the resurrection, there would be no life, no power over death. Hallelujah! It did not end in death. The resurrection is life. Yet, it did not end there either. Not only did He rise again, but He also ascended. Unknowingly, many in Christendom leave this part off the list, which limits the Gospel to a demonstration of power that is only available "before and after" the present age.

181

We need an Ascension Theology. The purpose of dying was to rise. The purpose of rising was to ascend. The purpose of ascending was to send. Holy Spirit coming to fill us was a continuation, a passing of His ministry to the disciples and to us. He did not just want to be a superhero to one generation for all time.

The Spirit of the Elijah is the transgenerational prophecy Jesus fulfills in ultimate fashion through the sending of Holy Spirit to the disciples—us and all who will believe. Just as Elijah went to Heaven and left his mantle-double portion—to Elisha, Jesus left us His super-cape, proclaiming that we would be better superheroes than He—receiving a double-share of the inheritance of the Son of God. He passed the torch of His life onto us. Just like the Olympic Torch's fire never burns out, so it was with the Holy Spirit's fire. It has been passed on from generation to generation, expanding, growing, and filling the cosmos.

RESURRECTION LANGUAGE

Jesus holds the keys to life and the grave. He commands us to raise the dead. His resurrection lives in us and creates atmospheres of life around and through us. Our language should display this belief.

OUR ACTIONS CREATE CONSTRUCTS FOR THE **BELIEF** IN THE **IMPOSSIBLE** TO **BECOME REALIZED.**

This demonstration is not done through wisdom-less boasting, but through clarity and conviction.

My personal belief that God raises the dead alters my paradigm when death appears. My first thought is always resurrection. This paradigm was on display at the fitness center I worked at in 2006. Steve Irwin, "The Crocodile Hunter," had passed away the day before after being stung by a stingray. When I came into work, I told two of my coworkers that I was bummed about his death. I then said, "I pray that he will be raised from the dead." One responded by seemingly ignoring me as if the questions of life and death were too big for the moment, so the best thing to do was to keep doing what he was doing. My other coworker looked at me like I was crazy, almost laughing at the idea until she realized I was serious." Their responses were genuine, as this was language that was out-of-the-ordinary. My declaration introduced them to a new way of thinking. For maybe the first time, they interacted with someone who wasn't fazed by the limits of natural laws.

We are commissioned to respond with life when the world faces death. It is something the world cannot overcome. Once all of man's resources have been exhausted, and all medical help is utilized, and the person still slips away... hopelessness sets in, accompanied by the feeling that all is lost. What more can be done, life has left and the spirit has departed?

THE FIRST AND THE LAST

The answer to the problem is Jesus. Remember He is the "Resurrection and the Life."

> Do not be afraid; I am the first and the last and the living One: and I was dead, and behold, I am alive forevermore, and I have the keys of death and Hades.
>
> Revelation 1:17b-18 NASB

In the beginning, we were all wonderful ideas inside of God's heart, which He chose to give life and animation to in the generation in which we live. In the end, eternal life is the continued cohabitation of our natural relationship with Jesus. When He is our first and our last, we enjoy coanimation with Him. Death has no residence in this place. The more we spend our lives in this place with Jesus, the greater our awareness of His complete destruction of death's existence in the universe will become.

OUR COANIMATION IN HIM EMPOWERS US TO REMOVE DEATH FROM THE LANDSCAPE BECAUSE DEATH HAS BEEN REMOVED FROM US.

JESUS IS OUR FUTURE, NOT DEATH.

WE MUST DELETE THE EXPECTATION OF DEATH FROM OUR MINDS.

We should live vibrant lives as those connected to the Eternal Life Source. In Him—who is in us—death cannot survive. Death is defeated and deleted forever!

> Which He brought about in Christ, when He raised Him from the dead and seated Him at His right hand in the heavenly places, far above all rule and authority and power and dominion, and every name that is named, not only in this age but also in the one to come.
>
> Ephesians 1:20-21 NASB

No one was before Him, and he is after everyone. Nothing is over Him. He is one with the Father, He has complete power, and all things are subject to Him. Ephesians 2:6 states that we are "seated right next to Him in these heavenly places," therefore we have access to His authority.

> I will give you the keys to the kingdom of heaven: and whatever you bind on earth shall have been bound in heaven, and whatever you loose on earth shall have been loosed in heaven.

> Matthew 16:19 NASB

We can open the doors that no one else can! We have His keys. We have access to all of His power. We have the power and the right to advance the Kingdom of Heaven in the Earth! Raising the dead is included. We have received life and are commanded to give life.

Jesus is the One who is in control of spirits when they die. He is the only One who has the power to return spirits to their bodies. He has given this power too. His will manifests in His desire for us to raise the dead. He would not command us to do this if He were not willing to respond on His part. He would not tell us to do something if he did not want to do it through us. His life is the life force of the universe, and this is the life that resides in us. When death touches His life, it is as far removed as darkness is from light.

WE MUST BELIEVE

> And without faith it is impossible to please Him, for he who comes to God must believe that He is and that He is a rewarder of those who seek Him.

> Hebrews 11:6 NASB

[Moses] endured as seeing Him who is unseen.

Faith is the substance of things hoped for and the evidence of things unseen.

...God who gives life to the dead and calls into being that which does not exist.

Faith proves that what we cannot see does exist. The world does not see life in death, but we know the Author of Life and have the power to restore life when death comes. So, should we look for death? No, we should look for life everywhere we go. And as we go we will find life even in the midst of pain, sickness, and death.

In him was life, and that life was the light of men.

He is the light of life. When He shines through us, His light enters the heart of men, awakening them from the slumber unto death. Wherever His light shines, death vanishes, immersing the dead in the Light of Life.

FROM DEATH TO LIFE

In 2002, Allessia and I were in Uganda on a two-month mission trip with our dear friends, Bryan and Mindy Jackson. We were deep in the bush during one of our outreach crusades, reaching the remote villages with the Gospel of Jesus. The day after we arrived, a little boy died of Malaria. The team went expecting a miracle and prayed for him for four hours. He did not rise up. Halfway through the ordeal, we did see his body respond as his eyes blinked and he jerked. I thought that was the moment, though he slipped away again. I used to look at this as a failure. And, as I revised this section of the book, I wanted to delete the story altogether. However, one thing I've learned over the years is that we must look at what God is doing, and not at what He is not doing. The celebration of the small becomes a seed for the realization of the big. Now as I look back, I am astonished because we spoke to a dead body and witnessed movement.

Bryan had taken a trip to Uganda the year before with our friend Avi. One day, they were in a service when a lady brought in her dead baby for prayer.

In an Eastern worldview, the supernatural is the first response to situations like this. Even if they were to try medical help, in many cases, it would've been simply unavailable. The culture has always had a spiritually driven lifestyle, which is why miracles seem to happen more often in Eastern nations. This book is designed to expand those who believe in the supernatural and awaken those who are not. In Eastern cultures, it's not a matter of whether or not the supernatural exists, it's demonstrating that Jesus has absolute authority over all the other spirits.

This mother had heard about the wonderful story of Jesus and went to Him as the answer. In the story before, the mother did not choose Jesus, but allowed us to pray when we offered. It is an interesting contrast of situations. No excuses though, no matter the circumstance, Jesus overcomes them all. I do know that invitation breeds expectation, and as Bryan's father prayed for the baby, life returned. They said the baby was white as life had left the body. As they prayed, it looked like the letting down of blinds as the color and life returned, starting at the head and moving down the body. Oh, my Jesus, how amazing you are!

Another woman witnessed the miracle and ran home to collect her baby, who had died the night before. By the time she made it back to church, the service had concluded. She found Bryan and Avi standing outside, and without words, simply placed the body in Bryan's arms. He did not know what was wrong with the baby. He said that is smelled really bad and looked like a dead animal. Sorry for the description, but this was the reality of the situation. The baby was stiff and did not move. They laid hands on the baby, commanding whatever was wrong to leave. Then he took the baby and lifted it up to Heaven. When he brought the baby back down, it was moving. Then he handed it back to her, and the child was now alive! They still didn't know what was going on as the mother excitedly left. When they returned to the USA, they told me that they thought God had raised the dead through them, but it was yet to be confirmed. Six months later, a member of the team returned to the village where the miracle occurred and met a young healthy toddler. They told him the story of the baby dying hours prior, the mother witnessing the resurrection of the first baby, and then bringing her child with faith for the impossible—the restoration of life.

Resurrection breeds resurrection. I pray this encounter breeds within you the desire to raise the dead. They weren't attempting to find dead people (if Jesus tells you to, then you choose how to proceed), but when death came across their path, they had Jesus as the answer. I choose to believe life in the midst of death. In the times I've had the opportunity to pray since then, I've honored protocol and respected the people involved. Raising the dead is something I believe in, and I have had many friends now experience the power of resurrection through their prayers.

Many people in the Kingdom have seen resurrection miracles. David Hogan's ministry in Mexico has seen over 500 raised from the dead in the ministry in the last 30 years. Also, Heidi Baker and her husband Rolland, missionaries in Mozambique, have seen over a 100 raised. Smith Wigglesworth and John G. Lake, have many similar stories. There are much more including Reinhard Bonnke, Curry Blake, TL Osborn, and on and on.

"NOT ON MY WATCH"

My friends, Randy and Lisa, raised a lady from the dead while dining in a restaurant one night. They saw some commotion and went to investigate, finding that a lady had choked to death on her food. The family permitted them to pray, so Randy knelt down and held the lady's head in his hands. The paramedics arrived and performed CPR. Finally, they stopped and said nothing more could be done. Randy stayed there declaring, "Not on my watch, you will live and not die." The scene went for several minutes as the paramedics began to just pace around with no hope. Randy was steadfast in his prayer, and after some time, she opened her eyes and looked up at him and asked, "What is going on?" She then sat up as if nothing had happened, to the surprise of all who were involved. They found themselves in a normal, everyday activity, revealing the supernatural activity of Heaven when all of Earth's resources had been exhausted. A son and daughter of God revealed the power of God in the middle of chaos as they restored the order of life to a dear woman, who was simply eating dinner.

"As you go... eat dinner... or whatever daily life throws at you... heal the sick... raise the dead..."

COANIMATION

When we believe what we speak, our words have clarity and power. They will not be taken lightly, nor fall to the ground. The voice of Jesus breaks the barriers of eternity, time, creation, space, and distance. His Voice resident in us. When we cohabitate with Him, our lives become a coanimation of His. Jesus only did what he saw his Father doing, and we will be found doing what Jesus does.

OUR EXTERIOR LIVES ARE A MEGAPHONE OF OUR INTERIOR LIVES.

WHAT WE SPEND OUR PRIVATE LIVES ENTERTAINING WILL BE REVEALED IN THE LIGHT.

When we cohabitate with Jesus in the hidden, we will coanimate and cocreate with Him in the seen. When we are proximate to His omnipresence, His omnipresence navigates through us. We have access to the Source of the Universe. We are children of the Most High. Resurrection power reveals our love for Him to the world. If our secret life abides in the center of the Source, the power of the Source will animate our voice.

ACTIVATION

Ask God what coanimation with Him looks like in your everyday life.

Ask Him how to do the things that you do as He would do them.

Ask Him what He would do if He had your daily routine.

After you write out what He shows you, then pray yourself into His vision for your life. This visualization will empower you with resurrection life in the midst of the circumstances you experience day to day.

Pray this with me: "Lord, may I be ready to speak life into every situation, even raising the dead. Grant me the grace, peace, and fire needed in the moment to step out and believe for the impossible. Jesus, I give you the glory and honor ahead of time, and I thank you for choosing me to bring life to those suffering from the effects of death."

DECLARATION

I believe that God raises the dead. I believe that Jesus rose from the grave and is alive. I believe the power of His resurrection lives within me, and that I am an heir of His ascension. I believe that my voice is a carrier of light.

RISE REVIVALISTS!

NINE

APOSTOLIC VISION

IF WE ARE TO **BUILD** WHAT **GOD DESIRES** IN OUR **GENERATION,** THEN **WE** MUST BE ABLE TO **SEE** AND **TRANSLATE HIS PLAN** IN THE **EARTH.**

Steve Bremner is a good friend and fellow FIRE alumni. We cut our teeth together blogging, writing, podcasting, and other explorations in the journey of life. I've been a regular guest on his podcast, Fire On Your Head, since 2008. The show has grown remarkably over the years as he interviews an array of leaders, teachers, authors, and influencers. He lives as a missionary in Peru with his wife and kids. The fellowship they are a part of, Oikos, has a strong focus on authentic discipleship.

We often Skype together to catch up on the lasted flavor of life or to dissect the latest "Christian" trends. It's great to have him as a friend on the mission field to keep my worldview in proper perspective and hear his hilarious stories as a Canadian in Peru.

One day, as we were concluding our conversation, I began to prophesy to him. In a vision, I saw the Lord give him a strategy to reach his city. His team would have this unique ability to relate to individual households in ways suitable to them. What works in reaching one family may have the opposite effect on the next, but they were tracking with the plan and made the adjustments needed to maintain effectiveness. I saw that they were able to see the pattern of how God would unlock the doors to each family. The sequence expanded as they ministered to different people groups in different ways, according to the uniqueness of each group. The ability to navigate by the guidance of the Spirit made this possible.

Then, God took me above his city, and I saw the grid of roads and building. The houses they would influence strung together to form a path through the city. Some of these homes were rich, and some of them were poor. They were all varieties and types of people. There were houses on highways and in the alleyways, including the famous, the nobodies, the leaders of the city, and the everyday folk. It was entirely random, with no distinction or class emphasized. In the natural, it made absolutely no sense, yet it was the wisdom of God.

He lives in Lima, which is a massive metropolis with nearly eight million people. The idea of reaching such an area seems impossible. All sorts of tactics could be incorporated, which over time, may influence the city. Good ideas are great, but as my friend, Jada says, "a good idea has too many 'o's' for a God idea." Remember, God's will is "good, acceptable, and perfect." Many times, in ministry or life, we settle for that which is good and acceptable, but stop before we capture that which is perfect.

The will of God contains all three components. What if we used this as a strategy to reach those in our influential zone? I believe God revealed His will for Steve and Lima in this prophecy.

My perspective from high above the city was reminiscent of my Sky Dream. It was like viewing a city map or Google Earth with 3D buildings. I watched a home light up with an orange color as if the building was illuminating. Next, another structure a few blocks away lit up too. It felt out of order, but I could sense that those in the first building influenced those in the second. The lighting of the houses continued in a zigzag path all around the town, like stringing lights on a Christmas tree. To retain the imagery, I drew out a city grid in my journal and colored in 12 houses. Then, I connected each house with a line, like a child's book that reveals a hidden picture when complete. The lines represented the Kingdom expanding from house to house. This path was random and unconventional. However, it was God's path through the city. Each house had the influence and keys to reach the next one on God's path. It was random in the natural, but a divine design in the supernatural. Father's plan to fill Lima, Peru with His Kingdom is already a reality in Heaven. Tapping into His plan makes it a reality on the Earth.

I encouraged Steve to view his ministry in Peru through this strategy, which will lay a foundation for the houses to be reached, from day to day, and generation to generation until all of Lima becomes adopted into God's Family.

How do you reach a city? Find God's path through the city, and you will find the hearts He will use to reach the ones in that city. In the vision, not all of the buildings were homes. They were businesses, government buildings, schools, parks, sports facilities, etc. The path was also just as significant as the buildings themselves. When I completed the drawing in my journal, it looked like a power grid. Without the lines—the path—the source of power would've been cut off. As the path continued through the city, it completed a full circuit. Heaven's power route formed. The path was the center of the city in Father's eyes. The connection of people along this route are Heaven's government in the city. One Family spread to become a "Family of Families."

At the time that I gave Steve this word, he was with a different ministry, which was two years before he met Oikos. After his transition, he discovered Oikos had a much different vision than the previous (traditional missionary) ministry model he worked with when he arrived in Peru. Rather than focusing on building a big church with hopes of drawing people into it, Oikos' approach to ministry in Peru is a discipling model that has a goal of reaching people from house to house. They set up what they call "missional communities," which are small groups of people in a house that meet together. When the group approaches ten, they start a new one in a new home. Oikos had the same strategy that I saw mapped out in my vision two years before. In reality, they were already there, functioning in this model. God orchestrated Steve to join them at just the right time in his life.

A large church may indeed arise out of this plan in the future, but the strategy was to follow the path. Large meetings and meetings from house to house are both Biblical. The issue is not of form. Dr. Gladstone emphasizes:

"YOU CAN CHANGE FORM AS LONG AS THE DAY IS, IF THE [MOVEMENT] IS NOT ON FIRE, THEN THE WHOLE THING IS WORTHLESS."

The plans from Heaven for Oikos to reach the city is to create a discipleship model. This strategy is not the dogmatic way to reach every city, but it is a way that God has given them to reach theirs'.

God's plan to take the city I live in, Atlanta, may be much different. Atlanta has a massive suburban sprawl. One of the ways to reach these communities may be through effective churches that are on fire with the plans and purposes of Heaven. Another plan of God is stadium ministry. They are all different pages in God's blueprint to receive the Earth into Himself. The point is to find out what God's path is and to follow it. You will discover his plan to reach your city.

The easiest way to discover God's path through your city is to fall in love with it. If you love them, then you will see the people as He sees them, you will see your city as He sees your city, and you will see His plan to reach your city. All the cities of the Earth are already His, they are just waiting for his sons and daughters to make it known, and construct according to the design Heaven intends for that city.

We would be wise to discover and follow the plans of God He has established for the cities of the Earth. If we find out what God is doing, then we will be much more effective in our ministries. The goal of this chapter will be to understand how to build something "sent" of God. If it's "sent" of God, then it will be an apostolic work. Therefore, the requirement for any work is to have an apostolic vision. I feel like the prophecy I gave Steve was not just for his ministry alone, but for all of us.

197

Steve found not just a ministry, but also a Family, then the vision for the city began to take shape.

ONLY THROUGH FAMILY—SONS AND DAUGHTERS, MOTHERS AND FATHERS, DOING LIFE TOGETHER—CAN APOSTOLIC MINISTRIES TRULY EMERGE.

To develop an apostolic vision, we need to prophetically understand how to see things in this light. When we understand the plan of God and what He is building in the Earth, then we will grasp our places in His plan and in our generation in a powerful way.

THE FOUNDATION STONE

Jesus is the foundation stone. He is the revelation of God to humankind. Everything in the church is built on Him, for Him, and through Him. He is the foundation for all creation (John 1:1-5). He is the spoken Word of God, who became flesh, and walked with us to show us the way to God, the way to live in the Spirit, and the way to fellowship as a Family, (John 1:14; 14:6; 17). He chose to have a body of people in the Earth to be His ambassadors (2 Corinthians 5:20), and preach the good news that He is Lord to all men everywhere (Matthew 28:18-20).

There must be a proper foundation in place for the rest of the building to be built upon and function properly. At the very beginning of the church, Jesus laid a foundation for us to think and operate this way.

> Now when Jesus came into the district of Caesarea
> Phillippi, He was asking His disciples, 'Who do people
> say that the Son of Man is?' And they said, 'Some say

John the Baptist; and others Elijah; but still others, Jeremiah, or one of the prophets.

Matthew 16:13-14 NASB

When Jesus asked His disciples who people said that He was, their response was a natural one. They knew he was supernatural, so they compared Him to other supernatural men. This response sounds good, but their vision was still on men and not on God. They needed to lift their vision higher, so Jesus asked them the question again:

> He said to them, 'But who do you say that I am?' Simon Peter answered, 'You are the Christ, the Son of the Living God.' And Jesus said to him, 'Blessed are you Simon Barjona, because flesh and blood did not reveal this to you, but my Father who is in heaven.
>
> vv 15-17

Peter fixed his gaze on God. He was not comparing Jesus to other men. Jesus was more than a man. He was God manifested in their midst—yet it still required the unveiling of a mystery to see this. Jesus' method of revelation occurred in this manner to show that the unveiling of the mysteries of the Kingdom come from God, not from man. The ability to recognize the depth of the revelation cannot be surface-level. It must be a sight that sees beyond the signal the eyes communicate to the brain. It requires the ability to intercept the transmission of Heaven to the Earth. Peter's answer showed that he was connected, empowering him to make the statement, "You are the Christ, the Son of the living God."

Peter knew to look to the Father because he was doing life with the Son. Through the sonship of Jesus, the Father was made known, causing Peter to turn his gaze from mankind to Godkind. He could hear what the Father said about the Son because he heard what the Son said about the Father. When we see the Son, we become like the Son. When we become like the Son, we see the Father the way the Son sees Him. Even though Peter had not quite captured the full revelation of heavenly Family, he had experienced enough to look to the Father as the Source to answer Jesus' question.

In retrospect, it is easy to miss the implication of Peter's response. From our perspective, Peter got an "A+" in Theology. What if we didn't know who Jesus was? What if we had a clue, but we weren't quite sure, as the other disciples may have felt? What would it take for us, to look at another man and declare with brave clarity, "Here is God!"? This is monumentous! Peter's answer released a clarion call throughout the Earth that God was present. Peter became a mouthpiece for all creation to recognize and return to their Creator. It was THE announcement to the universe, "This man is God."

Do you realize what it took for Peter to speak this out? What it took for Peter to confess this with his lips? Peter, who was a Jew, in a nation where all men were looking for the coming of the Messiah? It was a huge risk to look at this man, Jesus, as the Son of God. Yet, all the others overlooked it. God was staring them in the face, but because they were looking at the appearance of a man, they missed the revelation needed to see that this was the appearance of God. Peter's relationship with Jesus at this point had graduated from friendship to sonship. The disciples were still somewhere in-between.

> I also say to you that you are Peter, and upon this rock I will build my church; and the gates of Hades will not overpower it. I will give you the keys of the kingdom of heaven; and whatever you bind on earth shall have been bound in heaven, and whatever you loose on earth shall have been loosed in heaven.

vv 18-19

Jesus recognizes that Peter had a revelation of Him from the Father. Peter, in the Greek, is *petros,* meaning a stone or a boulder. When Jesus made this statement, He was standing in front of a large rock face at Caesarea Philippi. Jesus said, "On this rock, I will build my church," as He pointed to the rock face. "Rock," in this verse is *petra,* meaning a large (mass of) rock. He compared the single stone—Peter, to the large stone wall, which contained innumerable stones. Peter was a small rock, and on this large rock—the revelation that He was the Son of God—He will build His church.

Ironically, the rock face near where Jesus and the disciples were standing, contained a cave with a small pool inside of it known as "The Gate of Hades." Jesus wasn't just being metaphorical. He took His disciples to the gate of hell to reveal that He was the Son of God and that hell would not stand against those who knew Him as such. When our lives are lived in this revelation, all of Heaven is present within us, and none of hell is able to stand against us.

THE **REVELATION** OF **JESUS** IS THE **REVELATION** OF **SONSHIP**.

THE **REVELATION** OF **SONSHIP** IS THE **REVELATION** OF **FAMILY**.

The revelation of Family storms the gates of hell. The reason even "apostolic" churches aren't overcoming the gates of hell the way Jesus describes here is that they are so focused on being apostles and prophets, they miss becoming sons and daughters. Without learning to be a son or daughter, we will never become mothers and fathers. This revelation is one of the most important of my life, which came through learning to be a son to Leif Hetland and allowing him to father me into my apostolic dreams.

The very first thing to understand in the church is that Jesus is Lord. The way He revealed this was through His coming as a Son. This revelation establishes the church. If the foundation of the is revelation, then the rest of the building materials are also born through revelation. Only sons and daughters can hear from the Father like Peter. Listening this way requires the wisdom of the Spirit. As seen is the response of the other disciples, a zealous spiritual assessment through the eyes of man will not be able to form the image of Christ in the Earth. Ministry without sonship is ministry without revelation. Ministry without revelation is not building the body of Christ; it's building something in-between. It may have a form of godliness, but it will lack the power or the fullness thereof.

Sons and daughters are hardwired to intercept Heaven's broadcast. There are satellite dishes around the globe listening for extraterrestrial signs of life. Do we position our hearts in a similar manner to listen for the Father's celestial transmission? The Kingdom is built in us through relationship. Peter was introduced to the Father through Jesus and was able to recognize the Son and declare Him before his brothers. When our hearts are in a relationship with Jesus like Peter, we will identify what God is revealing and share with others what He said. When Peter declared that Jesus was the Son of God, he also revealed his own sonship. He showed that he could hear the Father's voice just like Jesus. An essential element of the Gospel is the flow from Heaven to the heart, and from the heart to the Earth. Pete's heart received the Heavenly transmission that Jesus was the Son of God. He rebroadcast this transmission by announcing it to his brothers. Revelation goes in, and it comes out when the vessel has become the revelation. Peter's sonship enabled him to see the Son. What is transmitted in, is transmitted out.

As soon as sonship is established, Jesus immediately begins to build His church. Jesus illustrates this perfectly in His conclusion of the "Sermon on the Mount."

> Therefore everyone who hears these words of Mine and acts on them, may be compared to a wise man who built his house on the rock. And the rain fell, and the floods came, and the winds blew and slammed against that house; and yet it did not fall, for it had been founded upon the rock.

> Everyone who hears these words of Mine and does not act on them, will be like a foolish man who built his house on the sand. The rain fell, and the floods came,

and the winds blew and slammed against that house;
and it fell – and great was its fall.

Jesus has set up our lives to survive on His words. Our lives should encompass everything He has said and is saying.

It is written, 'Man shall not live on bread alone, but on every word that proceeds out of the mouth of God.'

vv 4:4

The words He gives us feed our spiritual lives. They are the manna for our generation and the foundation for the framework of the church and the Kingdom.

GROUND LEVEL

The next stone of revelation given to build the ground level of the church was Jesus's revelation to His disciples of His Passion—His impending death. The revelation that Jesus is the Son of God who must suffer, die, rise again, and ascend is the centrality of the Message. [The rejection of these foundational truths is the basis for which most cults and false religions stand.]

He must suffer death from man to redeem man from suffering death. He came from God to man—as a man—to save humanity from the ways of man and restore them to the ways of God. His death by men will put their ways to death. In Him, they acknowledge that the way they have been living is evil (incomplete) and that they need a transformation into good (complete) living. Therefore, when we believe, we shift from living in the paradigm of men into living in the paradigm of God.

> From that time Jesus began to show His disciples that He must go to Jerusalem and suffer many things from the elders and chief priest and scribes, and be killed, and be raised on the third day.

> Peter took Him aside and began to rebuke Him, saying, 'God forbid it, Lord! This shall never happen to you.'

> But He turned and said to Peter, 'Get behind Me, Satan! You are a stumbling block to Me; for you are not setting your mind on God's interest, but man's.

> vv 21-23

Unfortunately, after announcing Jesus' sonship, Peter looks the wrong direction. His vision was on God for the first revelation, but for the second, his vision was on man. Peter did not understand that Jesus was building upon the first revelation. Sometimes we get one revelation just to set us up for another. The danger lies in camping out on the first and missing the second. Peter took his eyes off the fact that God was speaking with him and revealing something new to him. His heavenly response shifted into an earthly reaction.

The devil aims to get us to follow selfish appetites—something appealing to the flesh. There is nothing the flesh hates more than death. It would rather sacrifice the spirit than itself, just to survive a little bit longer, (just as Esau exchanged his birthright for a bowl of soup).

Jesus recognizes Satan influencing Peter because Peter's response was one of self. Jesus knew Satan's routine, who fell because the image of himself was more valuable than the image of God. The root of Satanism is the worship of self, not the worship of the devil. Self-attention will cause us to twist the word of God into something that satisfies the desires of the flesh. This pattern produces unredeemed thinking. Such a mental breakdown will cause us to rebuke the voice of God in our lives for something "self" desires, believing that we are led by the Spirit. Jesus exposes this by turning away from Peter to rebuke Satan. Then Peter's eyes open to the origin of influence that caused his reaction.

Self is an enemy of Family. It chooses to preserve the one and sacrifice the whole. Sonship chooses to sacrifice self for the sake of the whole—the Family. Family empowers the individual, which make the Family strong as a whole.

Hearing that his wonderful Friend, who was just revealed by God Himself as the Messiah and Son of God, would soon die, was too much for Peter to handle. His rebuke of Jesus was meant to save Jesus. Peter was still a son, but he was listening to himself now, not the Father. Jesus sees this disconnect in the Family, turns away from Peter, and rebukes Satan. I've highlighted His "turning" for the second time know to show that Jesus rebuked that which came from outside the Family. Peter was "under the influence" of an inferior voice. Satan has no place in the Family, so his goal is to try and rip the family apart. Jesus didn't call Peter Satan; Peter might have never recovered from that. No, Jesus rebuked the destroyer of families, whose aim is to disrupt Heaven's broadcast with the noise of self.

Jesus is building His church with a vision for the eternal. Eternal vision will sacrifice temporal comfort to see the plan of God impact future generations. Peter's vision wasn't eternal; it was temporal. He sought to preserve the "now" rather than ensure the future. As we know from history, the lives the disciples lived proved that they captured this revelation. We are here today because of they chose to live from the words of Jesus.

THE 5ᵀᴴ KINGDOM

The church is the Family through which the Kingdom of God is filling the Earth. The issue of the Kingdom was critical in the Jewish mindset at the time of Jesus. Israel was a captive nation looking for the Messiah to deliver them from their earthly bondage, which is why they missed His appearing when he came to liberate them from eternal bondage.

> The time is fulfilled, and the kingdom of God is at hand;
> repent and believe in the gospel.
>
> Mark 1:15 NASB

Jesus announces that the Kingdom that they were eagerly waiting for was here. Jesus was, of course, proclaiming this news to his Jewish kinsmen. An understanding of the Kingdom prophesied in the book of Daniel would have most likely been one of the texts brought to mind at such an announcement. The interpretation of Daniel's prophecy of the coming Kingdom was received through a natural worldview, even though it was a supernatural. The same mistake often happens today. Prophecy is by nature, supernatural, but many give it a natural reception. Such prophecies need the translation of the Holy Spirit if they are to be apprehended as God designed them to be. Jesus was revealing in Himself the true fulfillment of this Kingdom prophecy.

The theology of time was that the coming Kingdom and Messiah would drive the Romans out of Israel. The nation's circumstances caused them to dwindle down the marriage of Heaven and Earth—as illustrated in Jacob's dream—to a national or natural rescue. When Jesus didn't fulfill the Kingdom in the way they expected, His identity was misidentified. That which an entire nation desperately longed to experience was right in front of them but (initially) they were unable to see it.

Likewise, starting at the beginning of the World Wars, many began to develop a "rapture" mentality. They started to look for the fulfillment of Scripture through the lenses of their present condition. The conditions of a world war were so bleak; they viewed it as prophesied judgment. Theology surfaced that God would "rapture" or take the church away just before the "Great Tribulation." Today, this theology still exists, but the realization that God is good, and Heaven is already filling the Earth has opened the eyes of many in the church to the true nature of their loving Father. The same error the Pharisees made in their assumption of Kingdom fulfillment can still be made today if we look at the Kingdom as a natural means to an end.

The "Kingdom" as described in the Book of Daniel was much more than natural deliverance. It was a culminating Kingdom that would bring spiritual freedom as well. Extreme oppression, such as the Romans in Israel, or the World Wars can narrow the theology to meet the need in a way that was never intended. In situations like this, God always provides the answer. Israel was in captivity in Babylon when God used a very unusual way to reveal the coming Kingdom. He chose to give a dream the king who enslaved His own people. This king was Nebuchadnezzar, who also happened to rule the world at the time. The "highest seat" of earthly power was used to reveal the coming of the "highest seat" of heavenly power, which shows the importance of revelation, and how God can use someone who may be seen as an enemy to bring liberation.

When Nebuchadnezzar had the dream, he had no idea what it meant, and it terrified him. He was exposed to a world far beyond the immaculate lifestyle he lived as the King of Babylon. After a search among the wise men, magicians, and astrologers, and sorcerers, Daniel emerged to tell the king his dream:

> You, O king, were looking and behold; there was a single great statue; that statue which was large and of extraordinary splendor, was standing in front of you and its appearance was awesome.

> The head of the statue was made of fine gold, its breast and its arms of silver, its belly and its thighs of bronze, its legs of iron, its feet partly of iron and partly of clay.

> You continued looking until a stone was cut out without hands, and it struck the statue on its feet of iron and clay and crushed them. Then the iron, the clay, the bronze, the silver and the gold were crushed all at the same time and became like chaff from the summer threshing floors; and the wind carried them away so that not a trace of

them was found. But the stone that struck the statue became a great mountain and filled the whole earth.

Daniel 2:31-35 NASB

Then, Daniel interprets the dream for the king. He reveals that the different parts of the statue represent four kingdoms—head, breast and arms, legs, and feet. Their substance describes their rule and power. The statue itself represents the Evil Empire—all kingdoms standing against the Kingdom of God, across all time. They also represent three literal empires that would arise after the fall of the Babylonians—Medo-Persia, Greece, and Rome.

Next, he translates the significance of the rock striking the statue. The rock represents the King of Heaven. It starts out small, but hits the statue with such velocity that it shatters. This represents the shattering of the four kingdoms so that all that remains is the Fifth Kingdom—Kingdom of Heaven— that fills the Earth.

> In the days of those kings the God of heaven will set up a kingdom which will never be destroyed, and that kingdom will not be left for another people; it will crush and put an end to all these kingdoms, but it will itself endure forever.

vv 44

If we expand our scope and view this through the lens of Jesus, we see how the dream fulfilled through history. The Kingdom of God is the Fifth Kingdom that destroys the power, dominion, and rule of the Four

Kingdoms. The Kingdom—the Stone—is cut out without hands, which identifies that its source is not man-made. It is a Kingdom that enters the realm of the natural, having originated in the realm above. It strikes the other kingdoms and removes the rule of the natural order as it fills creation with the dominion of the divine. The natural mindset is swept away by the wind of the Holy Spirit. Likewise, the last of the natural kingdoms, Rome, was swept away, not through rebellion, but through the germination of the Gospel. Jesus did fulfill the natural expectation of Israel, but it came through a spiritual precedence.

The imagery of the stone cut out without human hands returns us to Jesus' illustration to his disciples about revelation being the rock the church is built on, and of which the gates of hell cannot resist. Jesus wasn't just giving His disciples a lesson on spiritual warfare; He was completing the plans of God shown to Daniel. Where does the Kingdom come from? From the revelation of Jesus deposited in the Earth. Jesus defining who He was to the disciples was the establishment of Daniel's prophecy. He is the Rock cut out without hands. His Family is the mountain that fills the Earth. He is revealed through us; we are His slingshots.

APOSTOLIC CULTURE

All revelation is a stone that both builds the Heavenly Kingdom and scatters the dominion of the Evil Empire. Anything "sent" from Heaven to Earth is apostolic because the culture of the Four Kingdoms is being replaced by the culture of the Fifth Kingdom. Heaven filling the Earth is the core of the apostolic.

How do we apply this to become apostolic in nature as revivalists? What kind of church makes an apostolic statement that is genuine, authentic, sent of God, and changes the culture in which it resides? And, where is such a statement being made?

THE **GOAL** OF THE **APOSTOLIC CHURCH** IS NOT TO BE **RECOGNIZED** AS **APOSTOLIC.**
THE **GOAL** OF THE **APOSTOLIC CHURCH** IS TO BE **RECOGNIZED** AS **JESUS.**

APOSTLE DEFINED

Simplistically, "apostle" translated from Greek means "sent one." The Roman Empire used "apostle" to designate a general who was "sent" to culturize a conquered country with the Roman lifestyle. If the way they lived their lives became Roman, they would never rebel, because the way of Rome had become their way of life. Israel would've been familiar with this term as they were subjects of Rome. Jesus assigned the term to his disciples with the purpose of sending them out into all the world to establish the culture of Heaven on Earth. The foundational call of an apostle is a culture-changer.

> And He went up on the mountain and summoned those whom He Himself wanted, and they came to Him. And He appointed the twelve, so that they could be with Him and He could send them out, to preach.
>
> 3:13-14 NASB

"But you will receive power when the Holy Spirit has come upon you; and you will be my witness both in Jerusalem, and in all Judea and Samaria, and even to the remotest part of the earth.

Acts 1:8 NASB

THE SIGNS OF AN APOSTLE

We have now somewhat developed an idea for the terms apostles and apostolic. We can now proceed to look at how they would function in the church today. The setting of the church is Family.

THE **CHURCH** IS A **FAMILY** WHO **CREATES** A **COMMUNITY** THAT **TRANSFORMS CULTURE.**

Imagine a gathering of superheroes, like the Justice League or The Avengers. If we ventured into their assembly, we would certainly be awestruck. The reality is that we are the supernatural ones. The miraculous is one of the primary characteristics of Heavenly Family and is ingrained our DNA. When we gather together, it is just as wonderous as a gathering of superheroes.

What makes a superhero super, is their supernatural abilities. I stated a couple of chapters ago that according to Paul, apostles transform culture is through signs, wonders, and miracles. These are the supernatural abilities of Heavenly Family. For a church to be apostolic and for her apostles to be true, the signs will be present. The sound of Heaven's heart beats at the core of those who function in the role of an apostle. They burn for the heavenly world to immerse the earthly world. Without signs and wonders, Heaven will not culturize the Earth. The fact that they are heavenly makes them different, makes them real. Their business card is the exercised demon and the healed body. All may not be functioning apostles, but all are designed to be part of the apostolic church.

APOSTOLIC COMMISSION

> But when Christ appeared as a high priest of the good things to come, He entered through the greater and more perfect tabernacle, not made with hands, that is to say not of this creation, and not through the blood of goats and calves, but through His own blood, He entered the holy place once for all, having obtained eternal redemption. For if the blood of goats and bulls and the ashes of a heifer sprinkling those who have been defiled sanctify for the cleansing of the flesh, how much more will the blood of Christ, who through the eternal Spirit offered Himself without blemish to God, cleanse your conscience from dead works to serve the living God?

> Hebrews 9:11-14 NASB

The writer is stressing here something that the Hebraic reader would have either accepted or vehemently rejected; that this Jesus is the fulfillment of the entire nation of Israel's existence and history. And that nation, while it remains unique as the people through whom he came, now must embrace the sending-out of the Kingdom.

Christ entered the eternal tabernacle as the Eternal Sacrifice. The earthly tabernacle housed the Holy Place. It was the place where the presence of God resided in the Earth. In Heaven, the Holy Place is God Himself, of which the earthly tabernacle was a shadow. Again, apostle means "sent one." Things that have their origin in God are obviously of God. The earthly tabernacle mirrored the heavenly. Whatever proceeds forth from God, is of God. Whatever "is sent" of God, is of God. If it has its origin from above, it is from God. A true apostolic ministry will mirror what is happening in Heaven.

Jesus chose the disciples as stones to "send" out into the Earth and spread His Kingdom. Just as the stone struck the statue, these apostles would be shot out into the kingdoms of this world to inaugurate a new culture, scattering the old one like dust. This pattern is intended to continue until the culmination of Creation—the realization of the fullness manifest throughout all space, time, and eternity.

THE **EARTH** WAS **CREATED** TO BE THE **RING** FOR WHICH THE **JEWELS** OF **HEAVEN** ARE **SET** TO **SPARKLE** AND **SHINE.**

The apostles didn't just adopt the Kingdom as the theology of their generation; they were transformed by the culture of Heaven. They became the message—inside and out.

NEW JESUS AGE

The Old Covenant was a temporal shadow of the eternal. Now the Eternal One (Jesus) has come, fulfilling the Old and inaugurating the New. The Kingdom of Heaven has come to the Earth through Jesus, beginning a new era. He broke the eternal veil between God and man and is the gateway through which we all must pass into eternity. Likewise, our relationship with Him allows eternity to flow through us. As an apostolic church, we are building, establishing, and equipping the things of God to all creation.

In many cases in the New Testament, the familiar phrase, "The last days" could be transliterated as the "New Jesus Age." "Last" doesn't always point to an end; rather it is referring to "latter," or the days after the fulfillment. Everything in the OT was pointing toward the coming Kingdom and Messiah. Therefore, we could say that "last days" meant, "in the days after the fulfillment of the prophecies of the coming Kingdom and Messiah..." "In those days, the new way of life will look like this..." "Days" refers to a new season or epoch. This epoch was essentially the New Testament or New Covenant, an era in which the rule of Jesus would fill the Earth with the culture of Heaven through his culturizers—apostles.

We live in the new Jesus age. The Messiah has come, the Kingdom has come. To see it, we must be born from above. We must live like it. The original design of God is revived in our midst as the culture of Heaven bleeds through us in the Earth. The prophecy's fulfillment is present age, not future millennium. If we believe the latter, then it will be like walking down a hallway to a door we will never reach. If we believe it is now, we will become it, and we will see all the world—all the cosmos—come to know the Father, Son, and Spirit—to know the Family.

APOSTOLIC FUNCTION & FIVE-FOLD MINISTRY

And He gave some as apostles, and some as prophets, and some as evangelists, and some as pastors and teachers.

Ephesians 4:11 NASB

For many years, as with most common reviews of this passages, I held the belief that in order for a church to be apostolic, then a ministry team with all five of these ministry gifts present within the members of the team needed to be present. A ministry team like this would be fantastic to sit under, and I do believe they are out there and will continue to emerge. However, I now view it differently. I don't believe that all of the roles of the five-fold ministry have to be embodied in separate individuals on a team in a locality to become something that is apostolic in nature.

Allow me to explain: I also used to classify these ministry gifts as offices, as with the majority of Charismatic theology. I don't think that is entirely incorrect, depending on what one may mean by it. I prefer now to view these as Kingdom influences within the church. We do need those that function in these gifts, as apostles and prophets are the foundations of the church and vital if she is to thrive as intended. However, I may have a leadership team that has a genuine prophet and a genuine teacher, but "oh dear" I am short an apostle, pastor, and evangelist. If this is the case, the team doesn't need to rush out and appoint people into these positions, that is not how the Kingdom works. What they need to do is look for the influence of these gifts present within themselves, and within the community.

The role of the evangelist may be present with several people, who when they come together, serve as the evangelistic function with the church. The focus needs to be on who you are, where you are at, and who Jesus is in your unique expression as a community of believers. The apostolic isn't a bunch of roles to be filled or titles to be given, it is a Heavenly Family that grows into maturity. And as a Family grows, the matriarchs and patriarchs will rise from within. They are culturizing mothers and fathers.

Apostolic fellowships are places that cultivate supernatural culture. Apostleship isn't achieved through name-tagging or making business cards; it's only discoverable in authentic relationships that are part of a Kingdom Family. In the way they relate to God, one another, and the world, you will see an authentic five-fold ministry emerge, with mothers and fathers functioning in the fullness of the gifts.

> To equip the saints for the work of ministry, for building up the body of Christ, until we attain to the unity of the faith and of the knowledge of the Son of God, to mature manhood, to the measure of the stature of the fullness of Christ.

vv 12-13 ESV

The fullness of Christ is our goal as revivalists within an apostolic culture. We must think apostolically in everything we do in life, be it our vocations, leisure activities, or spheres of influence. Our very lives will be Heaven's examples.

In adapting to this view as a lifestyle we can preface words or ideas, even things God has shown us with "apostolic." Some examples: apostolic fellowship; apostolic church; apostolic foundations; apostolic origins; apostolic function; apostolic expression; apostolic anointing; apostolic generations; apostolic lifestyle. The list could go on and on, but do you see how the dynamic of the word changes when considering it in an apostolic light? Each one could be a study in and of itself.

My stance is not a dogmatic statement on the "office" of an apostle. It is a personal revelation from my study on the matter that will hopefully help to bridge the gap between mystery and apprehension of the apostolic. The road is beginning to take route. If we are to affect our cities, revelation must be our weapon, our stone through which we abolish the evil influences in the area by establishing his Kingdom in the nations where we live.

ACTIVATION

Spend some time praying into your identity as a son or a daughter. Ask Father to express your sonship or daughtership:

How can you ignite your life through living from the revelation of Jesus in everything you do? Ask God for five steps to take to increase your awareness of his presence, voice, and Kingdom in your life. After you write them out, ask Him how these steps can develop and apostolic vision and culture in your life.

1.

2.

3.

4.

5.

Ask Holy Spirit for a strategy that reveals God's path through your city.

DECLARATION

I will be apostolic, sent from Heaven to bring the culture of Heaven to the Earth. I will not build my own kingdom, but I will offer up my life for God to build his Kingdom through me. I will keep myself with the goal and vision of attaining to and becoming the fullness of Christ in the Earth.

RISE REVIVALISTS!

TEN

KEY OF DAVID

DAVID FOUND **JESUS** INSIDE THE **HEART** OF **GOD** AND **DESIGNED** A **PLACE** IN THE **EARTH SUITABLE** FOR **HIM** TO **COME** AND **DWELL.**

The "Key of David" is a popular topic in the church today. Many authors and preachers have emphasized its prophetic significance over the last 20 years. Jason Upton sings of its relation to intimacy. Dr. Gladstone calls it "The willingness to live or die in protest to the law of sin and death." These are fantastic descriptions that begin to unwrap the concept.

Reading through David's story, you can find many keys I believe that unlock the secrets of David's fantastic life and testimony, which ring throughout both written and unwritten history. But what is the "key" determining factor that causes such a statement to be eternally and irrevocably made as "The Key of David?" The answer is a complex mystery that I do not claim to have completely unearthed. I do believe it starts with intimacy, which is the only door to unlocking the secrets of God. Such a life reveals the strength and resolve needed to live in protest to the forces who seek to destruct Family.

Intimacy is found in a life that is governed from Heaven and planted in Family. Leif Hetland describes this lifestyle in his book, *Called to Reign*, as living in "Chair One—from Heaven toward Earth." However, most Christians live in "Chair Two—from Earth to Heaven." The position of the heart in a "resting place" with God will reveal to us who God really is, then we will know who we are, and see the world the way God sees them. David had a Chair One lifestyle, revealing that intimacy was the key to his life with God.

Not unlike other revelations and mysteries found in Scripture, the identity of the Key of David is one that will continue to unfold and expand as the church awakens to her union with Christ. Ironically, the consumption of revelation breeds insight into new revelation. Becoming the old revelation allows ascension into the new. It's a relational vehicle wherein the more we know Jesus, the more we become like Him— dwelling in His sonship and basking in the secrets of His heart. The one who captures this paradigm has already begun to turn the Key of David.

THE APOSTLE KING

We know David as King, but have met David the Apostle? David was lovesick for God. It is evident in his Psalms and the Writings about his life. This relationship was infused with vision. As he looked into the eyes of God, he gained God's perspective on the world. As he leaned into God's heart, he could feel God's desire, bearing witness to God's feelings. He was so close that his gaze became God's gaze. Seeing the Earth from a heavenly perspective revealed the gap between the way God desired the Earth to be and the way it was. In recognizing this hiatus, David became the highway for Heaven to invade Earth. He began to build according to the pattern in God's heart.

His eternal legacy, even more than his kingship, was to be forever known as a "man after God's own heart." His heart drove him to become who he was. He would not be content to live on the Earth without transforming it into the image he had seen in the burning center of God's desire. The government of David's kingdom would be a heavenly structure that unlocked the dormant DNA of Heaven within the land of Israel. He was a king who culturized the Earth with Heaven, which is where we find the collision of kingship and apostleship. The foundation of Heaven he planted in Israel became the blueprint for the coming of Jesus.

THE SON OF DAVID

Jesus was the embodiment—the ultimate fulfillment—of this kind of relationship and way of thinking. He demonstrated the fullness of sonship in His relationship with His Father. As King, he brought Heaven to Earth, which was in direct lineage with David's kingship. David's life prophetically foreshadowed the ministry of Jesus. Why else would Jesus be described as the "Son of David"? Yes, they were paternally related, but it goes deeper than that. They were kinsmen of a kindred heart, connected by blood and Spirit. Jesus is the completion or full-unveiling of the life of David. All that David dreamed of was born as a living being in the Person of Jesus.

David's dive into the heart of God bred the need to extract that which he found there. Inside, He saw the King of Majesty dwelling in Israel. His need to build God a house reflected this. It foreshadowed and prophesied a day when God's presence would abide in the Earth. In gathering the materials needed for the construct, he set in motion a generational transfer that would not cease until God Himself appeared. Jesus inherited, as a Son, David's legacy of creating a place in the Earth for God to reside. Jesus picked up where David left off and once and for all finalized the project.

Jesus and David are forever linked because, if I can put in poetically, David found Jesus inside the heart of God and created a place in the Earth that would be suitable for Him to come and dwell. David's heart pulled Heaven to Earth.

David's kingship is forever, even when his sons chose evil because he activated Heaven on the Earth. Once this started, it would continue until the arrival of the King. From David onward, everything in the Old Testament was all about the coming of the King and his Kingdom.

David set a precedent for Kingship in the Earth. He would be the prototype of the coming One would fulfill everything. Jesus would be the archetype, the pinnacle, the One from whom all elements of the kingship and nobility would flow. David was the sketch; Jesus was the final product.

When we live according to the Key of David, we too will live in his heart, and our lives will construct the wonders we witness there in the life we live here.

As the gears continued to turn, Heaven and Earth became synchronized. David essentially reset the Earth to run on Heaven's clock. Looking back, we can see how it accelerated from David to his son, Solomon—whose own kingdom became Heaven on Earth to the kings and queens who traveled there. Over time, the Kingdom began to germinate. It wasn't outwardly visible at first. They knew they were in a season of heavenly extravagance, but didn't quite capture the eternal value because the mystery was concealed. It was a gradual unveiling throughout the generations by those who followed the pattern established by David. Many failed to capture it, even when diligently exegeting the Scriptures, but it was right there, hidden in plain sight, unlocked through intimacy.

"It's the glory of God to conceal a matter; it's the glory of kings to search it out."

THE **HEART** OF **NOBILITY** LEADS TO **REVELATION**, **REVELATION** LEADS TO **DISCOVERY**, **DISCOVERY** LEADS TO **WISDOM**.

Wisdom builds Heaven in the Earth. A heart attracted to the archives hidden in the depths of God will journey into the unknown. The nobility present within David drew him to the nobility present with God. Likewise, the nobility in the heart of God drew Him to the nobility in the heart of David. In this divine dance, God saw a man whom He could anoint as King and plant the seeds of revelation for His own Son to

225

inherit and reign in the Earth, as He reigned in Heaven. David's nobility activated him to become the vessel through which Heaven would travel to Earth.

Revelation is the establishment of the Kingdom of Heaven in the midst of the people. David became the revelation he discovered, which is how David became an apostle hundreds of years before it was given. He accessed the "coming Kingdom" in his current generation and lived in sync with its fulfillment.

The reign of David and Solomon revealed to the Earth the pleasure of living in the rule of Heaven's Kingdom. The Davidic-Solomonic Kingdom aroused the desire of the Earth for union with Heaven. The Earth began to groan for the reality of the King of Kings to walk upon its surface, eat its fish, and to drink of and walk upon its waters. Water turning into wine is an oracle to the upgrade that creation experiences when the sons of God arise. The expectation of a Davidic King became the atmosphere of the land. The Earth is eternally incomplete unless it becomes one with Heaven. David saw and experienced this union from a distance, and began to build accordingly. Solomon's wisdom set everything in place for the Earth to get a taste of Heaven in his generation. This is the kingdom Jesus reigns over. It wasn't an earthly system, but a heavenly rule that caused both the land and the people to flourish.

Jesus was the Union himself. And we, when we awaken to who we really are, we also become the union of all creation. We satisfy creation's desire for the sons and daughters of God to be revealed. When we are revealed, creation is united with its Creator, who dwells within us. Jesus took that which was inside David's heart and gave it to us, just as David brought what he saw in God's heart and gave it to the Earth. As we come alive, so do those around us, so does Heaven, Earth, and all creation. The seed within us is the spark that which fires the universe. Jesus chooses us to reveal his Father. When we beat with the rhythm of His heart, creation tunes into His frequency.

PROPHET, PRIEST, & KING

Through his walk with God, David became a prophet, priest, and king. The prophet speaks to people on behalf of God, and the priest speaks to God on behalf of people. A true child of God has this identity also as they have been transformed into the image of Christ—who is Prophet, Priest, and King in perfect manifestation. Now all of us have this divine access. Seeing David in this light, shows the extent of his revelation. He pulled this to the Earth hundreds of years before it was available. I can survey his life today by looking back. However, what if we draft off of David's legacy and pull the future into the present now?

David broke protocol because he saw a higher way of living—seeing what was to come, and in doing so, became it. Because he had the heart of nobility, he was able to function as both prophet and priest. My wife, Allessia, believes that David is the greatest prophet in the Old Testament because he lived out the prophecies that spoke of Jesus. He didn't just prophesy; he experienced the contents of the prophetic word, even the breaking of his body. His experiences gave weight, depth, and clarity concerning the Messiah. In becoming it, the path was set for the hearts of God and men to become one again. That which happens in Heaven happens on the Earth when God's heart beats within a man or woman. The heart of David on the Earth mirrored the heart of his Father in

227

Heaven. David saw the essence of Jesus--doing only what He saw His Father do. I believe the key of David is found when our hearts' only desire is God Himself. Before Samuel poured the oil on his head, before Goliath fell from his stone, God saw in this young man, way out in the field, all by himself, the heart of a prophet, a priest, and a king.

DAVID'S KEY

We can drop a pin at any point on David's timeline, and if we move forward or backward just a bit, we will find David gazing into Heaven to discover how he should respond to the complexities of life on the Earth. I believe this secret to David's life is represented by a key. This key unlocks, activates, synchronizes, unveils, and fulfills. Simply put, it is the key to God's heart. The depths of love are accessible through intimacy. It is a heart-to-heart connection. Intimacy empowers the protest. Protest emerges from feeling the burning fire in God's heart for Earth to unite with Heaven. I feel that between the intimacy and the protest, David found something. And I believe that this discovery will shed more light on the understanding of the "Key of David."

When a king possesses a key, it speaks of authority. Within his kingdom, there are no doors he cannot open, nor rooms he cannot enter. Likewise, there are no doors that will open unless he permits it. The king goes wherever he wishes in his kingdom. He has entry to all with nothing held back or inaccessible.

> He who is holy, who is true, who has the key of David, who opens and no one will shut, and who shuts and no one will open...

> Revelation 3:7b NASB

I will give you the keys of the kingdom of heaven; and whatever you bind on earth shall have been bound in heaven, and whatever you loose on earth shall have been loosed in heaven.

Matthew 16:19 NASB

Jesus demonstrated unlimited access to the Kingdom during His time on Earth. Nothing in Heaven was unavailable to Him. He had complete access to every heavenly place.

JESUS' MINISTRY ON EARTH WAS TO MAKE EARTHLY PLACES HEAVENLY.

David prophetically tapped into this reality, essentially paving the way for its manifestation. Jesus reveals that He is the One David's heart gazed upon, and that He holds the key to the heart of David. The connection between David and Jesus sets the precedent for the heirs of the heart of God to become the bearers of the keys of the Kingdom.

DAVID'S GAZE

With Jesus as our King, there are no limitations in this age because we have access to the age to come. His word in our heart is the mountain that is filling the Earth. I believe this is a revelation that David found out there by himself with his father's sheep. Then, as king, he would not just have a skeleton key for all the doors in Israel, but he found the keys to Heaven as well.

Then I will set the key of the house of David on his shoulder, when he opens no one will shut, when he shuts, no one will open.

Isaiah 22:22 NASB

What does it take to open and shut like this? Such power creates unlimited dominion. No land, city, territory, or planet are unopenable with these keys. And if Jesus Himself lives in us through the Holy Spirit, then we too can be like David. I believe the secret is in the life that David lived before the gift of the Spirit. Therefore, we have the ability not just to kill a giant, but to be slayers of giants all across this world.

David was a young man that spent time in his father's fields watching sheep. In the external, this seems insignificant. However, David was learning to lead. He took the task seriously and performed it with a heart of excellence. Even in this lowly role, David did not waste his time. He made the most of it.

In 1 Samuel 17, sits the massive story of David and Goliath. Suddenly, in the trenches of the story, David's secret life is exposed even to the king of Israel. What David had been doing privately for years when no one was watching, unexpectedly becomes the determining factor in the salvation of Israel from the hand of the Philistines.

Goliath had been taunting the armies of Israel for forty days. Saul and his army were afraid, hiding from Goliath behind some rocks. David was not in the army; rather, his father had sent him to bring supplies to his brothers. This day, he happened to arrive at the same moment that Goliath came out, taunting with his words of defiance:

I defy the ranks of Israel this day; give me a man the we may fight together. And David heard them.

1 Sam 17 :10; 23 NASB

Unbeknownst to him, this is the morning that Goliath probably should've slept in. Today, there would be a different reaction when he exclaimed his usual chorus of harassment. Today, his worlds would be heard by someone who accustomed to hearing the voice of God.

I picture David arriving on the scene gazing into the heavenlies. His attention was on God with a heart full of worship and wonder. Suddenly, something from this realm distracts his attention from Yahweh. He hears vulgarities aimed at his God and his people. To even see the giant, he must look down from his heavenly perspective. And, when all you have been doing is looking at God, Goliath doesn't look all that terrifying.

> Then David spoke to the men who were standing by him, saying, 'What will be done for the man who kills this Philistine and takes away the reproach from Israel? For who is this uncircumcised Philistine that he should taunt the armies of the living God?

v 26

I can imagine it went something like this: David says "Hey, what are you guys doing behind those rocks?" Then, as Goliath defies the armies of the living God, David hears him. He responds, "WHAT! Who is this that dares even to fathom that in any way that he could ever speak such unthinkables to the army of the LIVING GOD?"

When everyone else is afraid and hiding, I am sure that David's bold proclamations caused quite a stir in the camp. David was saying "Who does this giant think that he is?" And everyone else, including David's brothers, were saying "Who does David think that he is?"

Everyone else was so afraid because instead of looking at God like David was, they were looking at themselves. And in comparison, they didn't have much on Goliath.

THE LION AND THE BEAR

As the percussions of David's bravery echoed throughout the camp, it reached the ears of King Saul:

> David said to Saul, 'Let no man's heart fail on account of this Philistine.' Then Saul said to David, 'You are not able to go against this Philistine to fight with him; for you are but a youth while he has been a warrior from his youth.

> vv 32-33

Saul thought that David was just a youth trying to be brave. He compared David to Goliath, who, in the natural, was clearly under-matched.

> But David said to Saul, 'Your servant was tending his father's sheep. When a lion and a bear came and took a lamb from the flock, I went our after him and rescued it from his mouth; and when he rose up against me, I seized him by his beard and struck him and killed him. Your servant has killed both the lion and the bear; and

232

this uncircumcised Philistine will be like one of them since he has taunted the armies of the living God... The Lord who delivered me from the paw of the lion and the paw of the bear, He will deliver me from the hand of this Philistine.' And Saul said to David, 'Go and may the Lord be with you.

vv 34-37

Even though David was a shepherd on the outside, on the inside, he was a warrior. "Wisdom" would have told David to "cut his loses." Remarkably, this young man went out to rescue his father's sheep from both lions and bears, and he lived to tell about it. He did not kill them from a distance with a sling; it says he grabbed them by their beards and struck them in their mouths.

In the application for our own lives, this concept is fundamental and only obtained through intimacy. Only from having our vision on God day and night will beasts such as lions and bears become things to triumph over, instead of things to fear. If we cannot defeat the lions and bears in our private lives then how will we overcome the giants that strike fear in the heart of our generation?

DAVID'S ARMOR

After hearing David's testimony, Saul saw the warrior in him. Nonetheless, he was still looking at David, the man, failing to realize the KEY to David's strength.

> Then Saul clothed David with his garments and put a
> bronze helmet on his head, and he clothed him with
> armor. David girded his sword over his armor and tried
> to walk, for he had not tested them. So David said to
> Saul, 'I cannot go with these. for I have not tested them.'
> And David took them off.

vv 38-39

So, Saul tried to cloth David with the best armor that the age had to offer. The problem was that David was not used to fighting with the weapons of the age. He was used to fighting with the weapons of the age to come. Saul's armor did not fit on David because David already had his armor ON!

David fought with the weapons of God's arsenal and not the weapons of men. If David met Goliath on Goliath's terms, he probably would have had a much more difficult time. The problem for Goliath is that he ignored David's prophetic warning and tried to meet David on God's terms. David would not have been so bravely enraged if it were not for the heart of God beating in his chest.

THE SWORD AND THE STONE

> He took his stick in his hand and chose for himself five
> smooth stones from the brook, and put them in the
> shepherd's bag which he had, even in his pouch and his
> sling was in his hand and he approached the Philistine.

v 40

What is a sword? It is a rock that is cut out by human hands. What did David choose for the fight? Five smooth stones from the brook. Often, brooks and rivers represent the presence of God. A weapon formed in God's presence was his choice to win the fight.

What is the significance of the stone? It is the stone cut out "without human hands" that destroys the statue in Daniel. Presence is the revelation of how to overcome everything the statue represents.

I don't think it is too much of a stretch to say that David—because of his secret life—was able to draw from God's presence the revelation to defeat the giant. I go as far to say that in doing so, he opened an eternal door in which the Kingdom of Heaven invades and overthrows the kingdoms of this world. It has always been part of God's plan, but could it be that David is the first one to recognize that it was readily available? The spiritual construct surrounding David's battle with Goliath reveals the key to his victory and sets a precedent for the rest of his life and the success of his kingship.

David was not armed with a sword, which is man's way of doing things, but with a stone, which is God's way of doing things, illustrating the "Key of David." If we could see the appearance of David in the spirit, we would see David as the giant, someone well-known in heavenly places.

When Goliath saw David approaching, he mocked him, looking at David in the flesh as if he were a little child. David's gaze was on God, while the armies of Israel looked at Goliath. There were three different perspectives; faith, arrogance, and fear. Fear submits to the arrogant, but faith triumphs over fear, un-phased by the boasting of the arrogant.

David's vision made him aware of the unseen, yet overriding heavenly realm that dictated the battlefield.

> The Philistine also said to David, 'Come to me, and I will give your flesh to the birds of the sky and the beasts of the field.' Then David said to the Philistine, 'You come to me with a sword, a spear, and a javelin, but I come to you in the name of the LORD of hosts, the God of the armies of Israel, whom you have taunted. This day the LORD will deliver you up into my hands, and I will strike you down and remove your head from you. And I will give the dead bodies of the army of the Philistines this day to the birds of the sky and the wild beasts of the earth, that all the earth may know that there is a God in Israel, and that all this assembly may know that the LORD does not deliver by sword or by spear; for the battle is the LORD'S and He will give you into our hands.

> vv 44-47

David prophesied to Goliath that he was putting his faith in the strength of his weapons, which would result in his downfall. The prophetic word itself was like a stone being slung into the mind of Goliath even before the actual rock hit his forehead. David could have slung the rock at the moon, but it was always going to become a meteor of revelation that hit Goliath right between the eyes.

> Then it happened when the Philistine rose and came and drew near to meet David, that David ran quickly toward the battle line to meet the Philistine. And David put his

hand into his bag and took from it a stone and slung it, and struck the Philistine on his forehead. And the stone sank into his forehead, so that he fell on his face to the ground.

Thus David prevailed over the Philistine with a sling and a stone, and he struck the Philistine and killed him; but there was no sword in David's hand.

Then David ran and stood over the Philistine and took his sword and drew it out of its sheath and

killed him, and cut off his head with it When the Philistines saw that their champion was dead, they fled.

vv 44-51

The scripture specifically points out that David had no sword in his hand and used Goliath's own sword to cut off his head. The wisdom of this age will end up cutting off its own head.

Just as in Daniel the stone destroys the statue—the idol, man's way of doing things apart from God—the stone strikes Goliath and kills all that he represents. Two illustrations in Scripture, both decked out in armor, defeated by the stone of revelation, slung from the heart of God. David versus Goliath is the apex of human reason versus divine revelation. The dream in Daniel was the spiritual imagery of David defeating Goliath.

David's victory released the rest of the army of Israel from their captivity to fear. They rose up in a momentous fury, fueled by David's victory, and ran down the army of the Philistines. David started a revolution. They saw someone with Heaven in heart stand victorious. David may not have been crowned king in Jerusalem for many years, but he was king in their hearts from that day forward.

Will the sound of your protest echo through the camp? Will you shepherd your time and defeat the lion and the bear in the dark, so that you may stand boldly as a son of God in the light? Friend, David was a forerunner for you. Jesus has empowered us through his Spirit to take the land for His Kingdom. All of creation is groaning for another David, another son/daughter of God to be revealed and start a revolution!

ACTIVATION

Will you answer the call? Will you turn the key that opens the door to a secret life where you learn how to kill the lion and the bear when no one is looking? Will you find the vision in this place to put your eyes and focus on God?

Be mobilized, run to the battle lines like David. Invade the Earth as an army of Davids. Prophesy to the giants how big God is. Be revivalists that bring revolution to a captive nation. Be a revolutionist that brings freedom to a captive generation.

Lord, show me the lions and bears active in my life right now, and give me the heavenly strategy to defeat them:

Lord, show me how to engage my heavenly place, and daily rest in you:

Lord, show me how to live from Heaven towards Earth and turn the Key of David in my life and my generation:

DECLARATION

I will be a giant killer in my generation. Lord, give me eyes the find secret doors to the hearts of cities and nations. I will use the key of David to defeat Goliath and raise up other giant killers. In Jesus Name.

RISE REVIVALISTS!

ELEVEN

PROPHETIC MENTALITY

PROPHECY IS THE **VOLCANIC OUTLET** OF AN **INNER LIFE SPENT** WITH **GOD.**

I grew up riding on the back of my dad's motorcycle. I had my first ride at two-years-old. It was natural to me. I never feared for my safety because I had complete trust in my dad. For a time, it was our only mode of transportation. So, rain or shine, to get to where we needed to go, whether to school or the grocery store, it was on the motorcycle, which happened to be a 1977 Harley-Davidson Low Rider.

My high school graduation present from my dad was a Chevrolet Cavalier Z24, a small, yet quick little sports car. All my friends had cars like this, and we would often go for drives together.

My love for cars and the fact that I had ridden on a motorcycle for most of my life meant that I had no desire to get one when I turned 18. Many young men desire to start riding then, but I had "been there and done that." However, I had only actually driven a few scooters and a motorcycle once up to this point.

Fast-forward to 30-years-old, and my desires changed. My friends now were into bikes. My friend Jeremy also grew up on motorcycles and had ridden them most of his life. I started dreaming about getting a bike and riding with him.

Simultaneously to this, our friend at church, Gary, had a Harley Davidson Sportster he wanted to gift to someone. And, after talking with Jeremy, he felt like God told him to give it to me. Then, one night after a church meeting, he walked up and handed me the key, instructing me to come and pick up the bike. I was stunned. I needed an extra mode of transportation as my wife was using our car to get to work. I had been riding my bicycle to work, which thankfully, wasn't too far from our house. But, this also meant that I was limited to getting to other places. The motorcycle blessing would fill both a need and a want. God works all things together...

So, Jeremy and I went to get the bike. He rode it to his house, as I had no experience. I kept the bike there until I learned to drive it. I started out riding slowly around his neighborhood. Eventually, I started to ride it around the town. Finally, I was comfortable enough to make the 20-minute ride to my house.

It was a learning process because driving mopeds and riding on the back of my dad's motorcycle was entirely different than operating one. It was a whole new world. The handling requires 100 percent awareness of the bike, the road conditions, and what everyone else driving around you is doing. To miss any one of these elements, could result in disaster.

Over the years, I have gotten pretty good at certain things simply by looking ahead. If I drop something, I often catch it because I move my hand not to where it's at, but to where the object is falling. If I try to grab it where it's at, then it will be gone by the time I get my hand there. If I move ahead of it, then my hand is there waiting to catch it when it comes.

Likewise, by looking ahead, I've avoided obstacles in the road. I've developed a subconscious routine of knowing the roadside terrain, in case I suddenly need to maneuver. One time, I was driving around my old blazer when I came around a corner going 55 mph and the car in front of me was completely stopped in the middle of the road, waiting to turn. I veered off into the grassy area on the right and drove between the electric pole and the cable stabilizing it to the ground. I avoided slamming into the car because I was looking ahead. Good thing too, because I had a 200 lbs skateboard box right behind the seats. If I hit the car, there would have been 200 lbs of wood x's 55mph slamming into me. Ouch! Thankfully, I had surveyed the terrain sufficiently to make the right decision to avoid the collision.

When I started driving my motorcycle, this skill multiplied times ten. Seeing and being seen on the road are the most important things in riding a bike. Your position in the lane changes with the surroundings-what you see coming ahead, what's behind you, what's to the side of you—basically everything in all directions. To safely ride a motorcycle, you must develop the sight for it. You must be able to see what others are doing and know what you're doing. The response should instinctively bypass the mind. I did have some close calls, which generated riding with the expectation of what to do if every vehicle around me were to hit me. This mental aptitude prepared me for the ones that almost did.

FORESIGNT ENABLES SAFE NAVIGATION.

This principle is true on the roads driven and the roads of life. Looking ahead empowers me to make the best decision at the present moment. Then, when future becomes present, I have safely and efficiently navigated there. As we grow in awareness of the thoughts and plans of God, we will begin to see them intersect in our daily lives, conversations, and thoughts. Just as when riding a motorcycle, it is essential to look ahead a be aware of the surroundings. Similarly, we can engage the prophetic lifestyle.

I believe that we can apply this to every area of our lives: What is Jesus doing in us? What is Jesus doing in the world? How do these two universes collide? Learning to see this way puts Heaven at the forefront and we will adjust our lives according to God's plan. Having this kind of sight is seeing with prophetic vision. It activates our mind to think prophetically.

TAPPING INTO GOD'S THOUGHTS

God is always thinking awesome thoughts towards everyone on the Earth. One way I often describe prophecy is simply being able to transmit these thoughts to others. As I go through my day, I position the antenna of my heart towards Him. Tuning the station of my spirit to His frequency makes me readily available to share His heart with the one He is thinking about. Awareness of His voice is something that I've spent years cultivating. As I nurtured the transaction of heavenly thoughts, I became ready to share as Holy Spirit guided me to the ones who needed to hear it. Just like navigating the roads, the awareness of God enables us to navigate the spirit.

There more I activated this gift; I began to realize that I could also hear what God was saying over churches, business, cities, and regions. His thoughts are both micro—individual, and macro—generational in scope. Learning to hear His voice and prophesy to a friend is the first step into prophesying to a generation. If we plant our secret place in His thoughts, then we will understand in greater depth His daily desires for our world. The ability to find the revelation, to find out what God is saying in the midst of a situation, circumstance, or everyday life, activates a prophetic mindset. If we set our minds on God's heart, we can prophesy His heart to those who surround our lives. Navigating His heart is the process of learning to think prophetically.

Being able to prophesy is a wonderful gift, but using that gift on a consistent creates a prophetic atmosphere in our life. Such a perspective considers Heaven on Earth in every avenue of life. A prophetic person does not just prophesy, but also lives a prophetic lifestyle. As Don Nori articulates for us, "I am not looking for a prophetic word. Because Christ lives within and lives His life through me, I am a prophetic word to the nations of the world."

THE INNER LIFE

There is a book entitled *The Prophets*, by Abraham J. Heschel that I learned about when I was in ministry school. Heschel was a professor at Jewish Theological Seminary in New York. His work brings profound insight into the understanding of Jewish thought and worldview concerning the prophets.

Upon reading the introduction to the introduction, I stumbled across this statement written by his daughter, Susannah Heschel:

> For my father, the importance of prophecy lies not only in the message, but the role of a prophet as a witness, someone who is able to make God audible and to not only reveal God's will but INNER LIFE.[1]

This quote completely stopped me in my tracks. (You know a book is good when the "intro to the intro" already has your mouth watering.) The prophet is someone who can reveal God's inner life. What does that look like, what does that even mean? I think my spirit comprehended more than my mind. I had yet to plunge headlong into the depths of the book. When people look at those considered either by title or experience, to be in some way prophetic, the emphasis is generally on the prophecy itself, which is not wrong, but as Heschel points out:

> The significance of [Israel's] prophets lies not only in what they said, but also in what they were.[2]

The prophetic word is like a bottle rocket. We see its explosion in the sky, yet there is a place where its fire was lit. The word is the prophecy, the place of ignition is the heart of the prophetic person. Discovering how to spark the fire is the inner life—a hidden life—consisting of things not yet revealed. When the Bible introduces us to David, he was alone with his father's sheep, yet he captured Heaven's full attention. Hiddenness is where a prophetic word is born.

Being prophetic is not just the ability to prophesy. If you have the gift of prophecy, it does not automatically mean that you are a prophet. A prophet lives a prophetic life. That is his vocation. The Word of God is his being. He lives in a state of constant transformation from the inside out. The word spoken to him becomes him. David had a noble heart long before Samuel anointed him as king. The anointing simply pulled the kingship from the inside to the outside. Samuel connected with God's thoughts for David, pouring oil on the outside to illustrate what was already happening in the depths of David.

Prophecy is an illustration by those who've seen the inner-workings of God's heart.

PROPHECY AND THE PROPHETIC ARE THE VOLCANIC OUTLET OF AN INNER LIFE WITH GOD.

All of us may not be prophets, but all of us are prophetic to the degree that the light of Christ is shining through us. Remember the words of the angel in the book of Revelation:

> For the testimony of Jesus is the spirit of prophecy.
>
> 19:10 NASB

When we see Jesus, our lives become living testimonies of what He is like.

THE REVELATION OF JESUS IS THE ANTIDOTE TO THE HUMAN CONDITION.

THE TIME WE SPEND WITH HIM TRANSFORMS US INTO HIS IMAGE.

When we've spent time with Jesus, we don't have to announce it. It will be evident in the presence that surrounds us. The inner life is a prophetic life. There is a prophetic destiny for those whom God finds waiting for him in the secret place.

This exhortation challenges us to cultivate that fire:

> But you, when you pray, go into your inner room, close your door and pray to your Father who is in secret, and your Father who sees what is done in secret will reward you.
>
> Matthew 6:6 NASB

He longs to meet us in our secret place. It is where he prepares us to become the fire He longs to cast on the Earth (Luke 12:49). Here, He fashions into his image. If we have been with Him, then the world will see Jesus in us, just as Jesus said to the disciples, "If you have seen Me then you have seen the Father." His plan for His people involves His people. And we are called to be a people who dwell secret place with Him. What we learn here is what we will shout from the rooftops. If we indeed have a genuine and authentic word from the Lord, then this is where we will get it. It's about a love between a Father and His Family.

> Surely the Lord GOD does nothing unless He reveals
> His secret counsel, to His servants the prophets.
>
> Amos 3:7 NASB

Our inner life is to be cemented by His. When we get alone with Him, He, (in a sense) gets alone with us. This rendezvous is intimacy with God, an interaction between lovers. He longs to reveal more of Himself to us.

A truly prophetic person spends his time addicted to the inner life of God. Paul describes this in 1 Corinthians 2. In speaking of the hidden wisdom of God, Paul declares:

> But we speak God's wisdom in a mystery, the hidden wisdom which God predestined before the ages to our glory... For to us God revealed [the hidden wisdom] through the Spirit; for the Spirit searches all things, even the depths of God. For who among men knows the thoughts of a man except the spirit of the man which is in him? Even so the thoughts of God no one knows except the Spirit of God.
>
> vv 7, 10 NASB

The Holy Spirit reveals this hidden wisdom to us. She knows and searches all things, even the depths—the deepest part of God. Just as an earthly father longs to share his secrets of life with His kids, our Father in heaven longs to share His mysteries with us.

The more we dedicate our lives to the secret place, the more experience and wisdom we will gain. The supernatural encounters we have with Him that leave us speechless will, over time, become something we can articulate. The Spirit combines "spiritual thoughts" with "spiritual words," giving us the ability to make known on the Earth that which we have experienced in Heaven. When we testify of Heaven in the Earth, we aren't just speaking; we are bringing Heaven to Earth through our words. When we live a prophetic lifestyle, we summon Heaven to Earth through our actions. Our jobs, our spheres of influence, our neighborhoods, and our friends will all begin to look like Heaven.

The day-to-day life that they live with us will reveal more of Jesus to them. Being exposed to us is like being exposed to God because all creation groans for God's sons and daughters. Our revelation lights the way for them to enter the Family of Heaven. Their desire reveals why spending our inner lives with Jesus is essential. If we haven't been with Him, they will not be with Him. If we have been with Him, then the way we live our lives, the language we use, the way we conduct ourselves will all be little revelations of Jesus to them.

Lasting lovers or close siblings know the each other so well that they can finish thoughts and understand what they are thinking. They do this without even communicating. So it is with God and us as we spend time with Him and get to know Him better each day.

PROVOKED

When we live our lives in heavenly places, we become aware of the spiritual climate surrounding us. This perception helps us to identify the need of the moment and how Heaven desires to respond. We saw David's response in the last chapter. It was sudden and urgent because that is what was needed to win the war. Paul's observation of Athens warranted a different response. The strategy of the Spirit was to plant seeds of the Kingdom, which over time, would lead to cultural change. It was a city full of idols. Their search for God led to a construct of false gods who prophesy false realities. Paul's lived his life from Heaven to Earth. Therefore, he saw beyond the masquerade of these idols and knew what was really going on.

> Now when Paul was waiting for them in Athens, his spirit was being provoked within him as he was observing the city full of idols.

Acts 17:16 NASB

His spirit was being provoked from within him. His desire was for Athens to know the true God. He began to survey the spiritual climate by visiting synagogues and conversing with philosophers. The very fact that he was provoked was revelation that Heaven had a strategy to reach this city. Paul didn't fly off the rail and start destroying idols. Instead, he followed the wisdom of the Spirit. This led to an open door to share on Mars Hill about the resurrection of Jesus to thousands of people.

When we experience provocation, it is likely God sharing how He feels about the condition of the environment with us. Tapping into God's feelings is known as *pathos*. If God is telling us how He feels, then He will upload a divine strategy into our spirit that unlocks the His heart in the situation. Like Paul, when we feel provoked, the moment may be met with the momentum, which could be the assigned time for Heaven to invade our city.

Provoked can be defined as *taunted*. This adds dimension to Paul's experience. The idols were taunting him or egging him on. We can compare this to what David felt when Goliath taunted the armies of the living God. When David heard him, he could not hide from Goliath behind the rocks with the other men. By default, because of the residency of the Spirit, he was forced to take a stand! Forced to silence the voice of the enemy! Forced to protect his people! Forced to display to an entire nation that his God would deliver them!

If something provokes us, it is because we have the answer. Be provoked by sickness and heal it.

BE **PROVOKED** BY **DEATH** AND **RAISE IT!**
BE **PROVOKED** BY **SIN** AND **PREACH GRACE** THAT **REMOVES IT!**
BE **PROVOKED** BY **CHAOS** AND **BRING COSMOS** TO **IT.**
BE **PROVOKED** BY **SICKNESS** AND **HEAL IT!**
BE **PROVOKED** BY **HATE** AND **LOVE IT!**

David's provocation was to take an immediate stand. Paul's was to develop a strategy. Both fulfilled the purposes of God for that moment in history.

PROPHETIC CAPACITY

When we see what God designed the earth to look like, we will have the prophetic capacity to fulfill the plan of God for our generation. The tale of prophetic life is one that spends a lifetime in this place. Who they are in public is a reflection of who they are in private with God. Their stature and their words are the embodiment of God's inner life. Ministry is just the result of a life of prayer. Those who spend the time here become prophetic.

When we have a legacy in Heaven, Earth around us will begin to terraform to the design of God for creation. A Heaven on Earth lifestyle revives God's original intention for people, places, and cities. A revivalist activates these plans. When our lives prophesy Heaven on Earth, we have captured the heart of the prophetic lifestyle.

ACTIVATION

Ask God three things He thinks about you:

1.

2.

3.

Now, as you go throughout your day, ask God what He feels about those you encounter. Learning to hear God is essential in the operation of the prophetic gifts. My book, *Activating a Prophetic Lifestyle*, is all about how to recognize the ways God speaks to you and through you. Once you've finished learning about the lifestyle of a revivalist in this book, it will help you take the next step in walking it out.

DECLARATION

I declare that I will prioritize intimacy with Jesus. My outer life will become a reflection of the majesty I discover through the inner life I spend in the presence of God. I will see my generation with heavenly eyes and craft my life through the plans of God.

RISE REVIVALISTS!

NOTES

[1] Abraham J. Heschel, *The Prophets*, (New York: Harper Collins 2001), p xiii. *Emphasis mine.*

[2] Ibid. p xxi

TWELVE

BURNING BUSHES

WITHOUT REALIZING IT, **MOSES WALKED OFF** THE **EARTH** AND **FOUND** HIMSELF **STANDING** ON **OTHERWORLDLY GROUND.**

What did Moses really see when he stumbled across the burning bush? The bush was on fire, but it was not consumed. It uncharacteristically befriended the flame. Two elements that would ordinarily be at odds we found coexisting together. Typically, fire pulls all the life-giving components from the bush in order to continue its burning.

So, what did Moses experience? What captured his attention? He saw deeper than a bush on fire without burning up. He saw beyond natural sight. He saw into the matrimony of Heaven-kissing the Earth through this majestic illustration God orchestrated for him. He saw the invitation carried by the flame. Something deep in his heart responded.

God spoke at the reception of the invitation. This moment was the conception of a new man.

Moses, in essence, saw what he was called to be—on fire with God. The presence of the Lord would literally be on him burning with supernatural fire the same way the fire was on the bush.

> The angel of the Lord appeared to him in a blazing fire from the midst of a bush; and he looked, and behold, the bush was burning with fire, yet it was not consumed.
>
> So Moses said, 'I must turn aside now and see this marvelous sight, why this bush is not burned up.'
>
> When the Lord saw that he turned aside to look, God called to him from the midst of the bush and said, 'Moses, Moses!' And he said, 'Here I am.'
>
> Then He said, 'Do not come near here; remove your sandals from your feet, for the place on which you are standing is holy ground."
>
> He said also, 'I am the God of your fathers, the God of Abraham, the God of Isaac, and the God of Jacob,' Then Moses hid his face, for he was afraid to look at God.
>
> Exodus 3:2-6 NASB

HOLY GROUND

Without realizing it, Moses had walked off the Earth. Suddenly, he was standing in a heavenly place. In a moment, a flash, "a twinkling of the eye," he was caught up into the presence of God. He was simply doing his day-to-day work of shepherding his father-in-law's sheep, as he had been doing for 40 years. However, this day marked the intersection between his history and his destiny. Today was the day of his immersion, his becoming, and his transformation. He had incubated a dream for eighty years that was now about to become a reality. The God of his forefathers "out there," and the God felt in his heart, had finally become one before him. No matter how disconnected he felt from his dreams, he was always accelerating towards their fulfillment. God was waiting for his heart to ripen at this precise point in time.

Any ground that comes into contact with the presence of the Lord becomes holy ground. Remember, holy is defined as otherworldly. The feet of the Lord essentially baptize the land upon which they touch. Again, His Presence makes the earthly places heavenly. Moses found himself standing before the presence of the Lord burning in the midst of the bush—a natural element immersed in a supernatural element.

God calls Moses by his name as a father calling for his son. Moses' identity was now affirmed, empowering him to stand in God's presence. Next, God instructs Moses to take off his sandals because he was standing on holy (otherworldly) ground. The instruction was so Moses could have direct contact with Heaven on Earth. God wanted no separation between Himself and Moses. This established intimacy in their relationship. Moses wasn't just being summoned to look at the fire. He was supposed to feel the fire, to experience the fullness of the fire, and ultimately, become the fire. The sandals represent any natural thing that would create a barrier between God and Moses (His people). His intention was for Moses to fully know Him just as He knows Moses fully.

Moses was having a transferable encounter. It was something he was to pass on. The only way it could only happen is if he knew what it felt like to be standing in Heaven and on the Earth at the same time.

We see the fullness of this encounter in the life of Jesus. John the Baptist prophesies of Jesus coming to baptize with fire.

> As for me, I baptize you with water for repentance, but He who is coming after me is mightier than I, and I am not fit to remove his sandals; He will baptize you with the Holy Spirit and fire.
>
> Matthew 3:11 NASB

> John answered them, "I baptize with water, but among you stands one you do not know, even he who comes after me, the strap of whose sandal I am not worthy to untie.
>
> John 1:26-27 ESV

In the mind of the Jewish listener, there would be a connection between what John was describing and the burning bush. Interestingly, John also uses "sandals" in relation to something burning with the presence of God. This time it would be slightly different. Moses was asked to remove his sandals: John was unworthy to untie Jesus' sandals. The implication is that the One who was burning in the bush was here in the flesh. The ground was holy because the Person in the bush was holy. John was declaring that the One who was coming after him is the same as the one who lit the bush on fire. This connection created a visual for the kind of baptism John was introducing. One could not light something on fire unless it was the kind of heavenly fire that doesn't reduce the element it is burning. Water baptism was a prophetic image that prophesied what fire baptism would entail. John essentially declares that the greater one will baptize them with fire just like the burning bush. He would not need to remove his sandals because He Himself was the Source of the heavenly fire. Therefore, everywhere he would step would become holy.

When Moses encountered the burning bush, he had to reprogram his mind to think heavenly in order to capture the call set before him. The burning bush was his new identity. He would bring the encounter of the bush to Egypt and to Israel.

HE WAS NOW A BURNING ONE IN THE EARTH, CONSTRUCTING HEAVEN EVERYWHERE HE WENT.

This story is such a prophetic picture for the ages. It is a picture of who we are called to be as well—immersed in fire like the burning bush, like Moses, and like Jesus. I imagine that every time Moses went out with his sheep, his destiny reverberated within him. He knew the day would come. He was able to see beyond the natural when he encountered the bush because his focus remained on God.

WE MUST BE CONSUMED WITH GOD IF WE WANT TO BE CONSUMED BY GOD.

The fire is the substance of the supernatural life. After the encounter, Moses demonstrated God to the rulers of the Earth and his people. This was a prophetic glimpse into that which was to come, the baptism of the Holy Spirit.

IMMERSED

Baptism means immersion. Baptism in water is immersion in water. In the original language, it means to be dunked under or drenched. It is supposed to kill you, but since Jesus died that death for you, you are allowed to come up, surfacing into a new life. It is not just a sprinkle. It is an immersion, a total covering from head to toe. You're wet, soaked, and saturated. If water is the substance of life in the natural, and it is what we are to be soaked in, then the Holy Spirit fire is the substance of life in the spirit, and what we are to be soaked in.

TRANSFORMING DNA

> As for me I baptize you with water for repentance, but He who is coming after me is mightier than I, and I am not fit to remove His sandals; He will baptize you with the *Holy Spirit Fire*.
>
> Matthew 3:11 *paraphrase*

Notice in the paraphrase of this verse that I removed the word "and," which is normally found in this verse between *Holy Spirit* and *fire*. There is no "and" in the Greek. Many teach that there are two baptisms described here- the Baptism of the Holy Spirit and the Baptism of Fire. Maybe, but I mostly disagree. I think the verse is articulating a higher echelon of experience.

Recent studies in quantum physics suggest that there are strings of vibrating light known as "string theory," which is the micro-fabric of all things in the universe. If we apply this paradigm to the immersion of the

Holy Spirit, it expands our understanding of the experience. Holy Spirit could be transliterated as "Otherworldly Breath of Life." Holy Spirit gives life to everything, sustains everything, and reveals Jesus to/in everything. If all things are vibrating strings of light, then the Baptism of the Spirit immerses these light strings into the fire of the Otherworldly Breath of Life. The Baptism of the Spirit changes us on the micro level—from the inside out—into the fiery image of God. Could this be how the bush was on fire and not consumed? The DNA of the bush was changed to a higher reality. Burning became its natural state of existence. Likewise, when we are baptized in the Spirit, our DNA is transformed into a higher reality, and burning becomes our natural state of existence.

Often, when Moses would go into the presence of the Lord, he would come out with his face glowing so brightly that he had to wear a veil for the people to look at him. Moses would also meet with the Lord face-to-face. What you behold you become. When we see Jesus, as Moses saw the Lord, we will become what we behold. Jesus has eyes of fire. When we look into His eyes, our eyes become fire.

MEETING WITH GOD UNLOCKS THE TRUE DESIGN AND SUPERNATURAL CAPACITY OF THE HUMAN BODY.

When Jesus transfigured, His entire body, even His clothes, were immersed in light to the degree that they became the light. Seeing Jesus transfigure created a framework for the disciples to know what it would be like when Jesus sent His Spirit foreshadowing their baptism of fire on the day of Pentecost. Without it, they could not become everything Jesus had called them to be, nor would they be able to do everything that Jesus had called them to do. They had to wait for the Holy Spirit to descend upon them. Once immersed in fire, they became the fire. They became the source, the torch of Heaven's flame. The Gospel spread like fire in the book of Acts by burning men and women who had become burning bushes.

THE LANGUAGES OF HEAVEN

Unlike the outer immersion of water, which only covers the skin, when baptized in the Spirit, the immersion of fire is inside and out. If you put a towel in water, it doesn't just get wet on the outside. When you squeeze it, water doesn't just drip off the edge; it pours from the inside out. The fabric itself filled with water upon its immersion. When baptized in the Spirit, we are sopping wet just like the towel. You could ring us out, and we would be dripping with the very presence of God. Every fiber of our being comes into contact with and is changed by the fire. We begin to vibrate with the frequency of Heaven. It transforms the way we live our lives, our interaction with people, and even the way we speak. The living fire is itself the God strand of DNA activated within us.

One of the reasons why the disciples first spoke in new languages when they were baptized in Holy Spirit fire is because the change in their DNA activated their reception of the language of the Divine. Holy Spirit could now speak the mysteries of Heaven to them and through them. Whether through earthly dialects or heavenly, they were now vessels of Heaven on Earth able to both communicate and demonstrate the Kingdom.

This paradigm gives insight into the significance of speaking in tongues—the languages of Heaven. The baptism in the Spirit is more than just speaking a few words in tongues. It's a new life in the Spirit. Because of the confusion surrounding this gift, the fullness of it has yet to be seen.

Some consider an insignificant or entry-level gift, but I couldn't disagree more. It is attacked because it is so powerful. The heavenly mind can speak the divine language, but it makes no sense to the earthly mind. Therefore, shame can try to attach itself to those who experience it. The understanding and development of the gift is hindered when earthly mindsets try to dissect it.

In many places where it is accepted, they have only gone ankle deep in the revelation and power that it contains. When a baby learns to speak, they usually start by mimicking basic sounds they hear from their parents. These sounds begin to be associated with different things in their world. The sounds become syllables, the syllables become words, and the words become sentences. I've seen many with the gift of speaking in tongues never progress past the sounds or syllables. Essentially, they speak "heavenly baby." Growth in the gift is vital. Why stop at the ABC's when there are whole heavenly languages to be discovered?

Another common trait I see that surrounds this gift is that many only have a one-time experience. I took two years of French in high school, but now I can just remember a couple of words and phrases. I, by no means, can speak French. However, if you ask certain people if they are baptized in the Spirit, they will say yes, but they only spoke a few words one time, probably many years ago. This is not a criticism. It is an announcement that there is more and an invitation to experience it. The gift of speaking in tongues is a powerful tool. It is not just a one-time experience. It should be a gift we use daily to build ourselves up in faith. It is an ongoing supernatural encounter.

This gift will grow the more we use it. ABC's will turn into sentences. The sentences turn into languages- with different tones and dialects.

Don't stay at the elementary level, when God has Ph.D.'s waiting to be given out.

SPEAKING IN TONGUES IS THE MYSTICAL LANGUAGE OF HEAVENLY FAMILY.

Language isn't understood unless its known or translated. Learning a new language requires constant practice, speech, and interaction. To unlock the depths of tongues, the same disciplines apply. Those who understand the language have the gift of interpreting tongues. I believe it's not left to be a mystery alone, but its fully comprehendible in the Spirit when the spirit and the mind are in union—again, combining spiritual thoughts with spiritual words. Tongues isn't only other earthly languages as some suggest. If that were true, earthly translators would suffice. However, it is clear that heavenly translation comes through spiritual insight. Interpretation of tongues, prophecy, and words of knowledge are needed to translate the gift when it's in heavenly dialect.

Speaking in tongues is the language of the Spirit. Don't just wait for the "utterance." It is your gift, use it whenever you want, and use it often. Paul said that he prayed in tongues more than everyone. Can we not outdo him? I think he would want us to. If we are on fire, we will speak in tongues.

THE GIFT OF TONGUES IS THE CRACKLING SOUND OF A BURNING HEART.

God spoke to Moses out of the burning bush. It was not the bush alone speaking, but God speaking through the bush. When we speak in tongues, when we prophesy, and when we preach the Gospel it is God speaking through us.

God commissioned Moses to go and speak to Pharaoh, but he was afraid. What he didn't realize was that he would be like the burning bush speaking to Pharaoh. Our commission is the same today. Jesus said not to worry about what we would speak, but the Holy Spirit would give us the words we need in the moment. If God can speak through a bush, then He can surely speak through us.

Voice is a result of breath vibrating vocal chords. The articulation of a voice contains the substance of Heaven when we are baptized in the Spirit. Our voices, whether speaking heavenly languages or earthly languages, contain fire. This is why we guard what we say. Our voices have become holy.

OUR VOICES HOUSE THE HEAVENLY, THE OTHERWORLDLY, THE VERY PRESENCE OF GOD.

With the Spirit in our breath, we are able to speak to the dead and watch them rise, speak to the sick and watch them heal, and speak to the outcast and call them home. Speaking the language of Heaven in the Earth causes our internal and external environments to vibrate with the frequency the Spirit, transforming the atmosphere to become one suitable for burning. Our inner life of burning will immerse those in outer lives with the substance it contains. It's a transfer of DNA.

MARVELOUS SIGHT

Moses was in the desert shepherding his flock when he encountered the burning bush. John was in the desert, shepherding his flock when he encountered the Burning Man. The world is in the desert, and they will encounter us, the burning ones. We are the burning Family.

> So Moses said, 'I must turn aside now and see this
> marvelous sight, why this bush is not burned up.'

Exodus 3:3 NASB

Neither did the bush burn up, nor did the fire go out. A "fire that remains" captured Moses' attention. The same fire that remains will also capture the world's attention. It's an intimately fueled balance. If we neither burn up nor burn out, the world will turn and see the fire that remains in us. It is an out-of-this-world encounter. When they encounter us, it is supposed to be otherworldly, heavenly, fiery, and Jesus-like. The world may see Christians, but only when we are on fire, when we are burning bushes, will their gaze behold a marvelous sight.

We have access to all the fullness of life and union with the Father. We have access to the fullness of His Family, His fellowship, and the fullness of His ministry. We have access to the supernatural substance that makes the bush burn and Jesus illuminate the Earth.

> I have come to cast fire upon the earth; and how I wish it
> were already kindled. But I have a baptism to undergo,
> and how distressed I am until it is accomplished!

Luke 12:49-50 NASB

Just as Father sent Moses to cast fire on Egypt, Jesus sends us as the His fire to cover the Earth.

And when I came to you brethren I did not come with superiority of speech or of wisdom, proclaiming to you the testimony of God. For I determined to know nothing among you except Jesus Christ and Him crucified.

I was with you in weakness and in fear and in much trembling, and, my message and my preaching were not in persuasive words of wisdom, but in demonstration of the Spirit and of power, so that your faith would not rest on the wisdom of men, but on the power of God.

1 Corinthians 2:1-5 NASB

Evangelism is utterly supernatural. Philip is the only one listed as an evangelist in Scripture, and his entire ministry was otherworldly. He demonstrated the power of God, translocated, and raised up a prophetic family. True evangelism, by default, is always supernatural. When we demonstrate a marvelous God through marvelous love and marvelous power, the world will see a marvelous sight.

BEHOLDING THE MARVELOUS ONES AWAKENS CREATION TO A BRAND NEW MARVELOUS EXISTENCE.

The fire in us is the Holy Spirit. The Holy Spirit is the Giver of Gifts who dwells inside of us and empowers us to present the Kingdom to the world.

OFTEN, IN THE **NEW TESTAMENT,** THE **PREACHING** IS SIMPLY AN **EXPLANATION** OF THE **MANIFESTATIONS** OF THE **SPIRIT OCCURRING** AMONG THE **PEOPLE.**

Moving in power and demonstrating the Kingdom is our natural programming. It is us, just being ourselves. When we live life in the Spirit, this becomes the framework of our personalities. Our natural response to sickness becomes healing. Our natural response to the impossible is to make it possible. We are naturally superheroes and heroines.

When I was a young believer, I used to think to myself in a robotic tone, "I have to e-v-a-n-g-e-l-i-z-e now." Then I would put on my "evangelism hat" and try to function in a matter that "witnessed" to people. "Hey man, Jesus loves you, OK bye," I would proclaim nervously before running off. I have to say that I did not see much fruit. To be honest, I was doing something I hated, not something that I delighted in. God is not a taskmaster. He is a lover. And out of that love, He equips us to become lovers and gives us the power to prove His love to creation.

Supernatural evangelism should be natural to us. In our daily lives, it is just who we are. In being myself, I don't have to put on my evangelism hat. I easily share who I am with those around me. It may be done either overtly, or covertly. I do it in conversations, or in healing, or in prophesying, and the list goes on. I am a son of the King. His entire Kingdom is at my disposal. When I can talk about the marvelous wonders of my King and His kingdom by allowing them to "taste and see" through my life, then I have evangelized.

Once, at one of the gyms I managed over the years, one of the employees came into work after school. He walked into the office and told me they had studied evolution that day. Understandably, he had some questions for me. "How could God be real if science and evolution conclude A, B, and C?" My response was simple. I told him how God created us to be with Him and how much He loves us. I didn't argue details. Instead, I shared the love of God with him.

We didn't get too far in our conversation before the presence of God began to fill the office. "He's here," I said. "Do you feel Him?"

Wide-eyed, he acknowledged that he felt God. Then, the presence became so heavy that he stumbled back into the desk and had to lean against it to stay on his feet. As this happened, he began to shake and tremble in God's presence.

When he came in, his faith in God was shaken, but he went out, his faith was stronger than it had ever been. His questions were met with Presence. He encountered a burning bush—a marvelous sight—and gained a marvelous touch from the Lord. The love of God was tangible, marking him with a multi-sensory encounter.

I did not try to work up God or manifest presence. I did not try to preach. I merely shared naturally out of the overflow of the fires that burn in my heart. When we do this, those fires inside us come to the surface and set others on fire.

A VISION OF FIRE

My friend Brandon had a vision at a youth retreat one night in the late 1990's, which created a framework in my spirit for the elements covered in this chapter. Often, we get prophetic glimpse years before the fullness of the revelation comes, preparing us to receive the personification of the revelation.

We had a glorious encounter in God's presence the night he had the vision. The power of Heaven filled the place, and the young men and women were lying all over the floor, unable to stand in the weight of God's glory. The experience was likened to the youth encounter in chapter one.

During the prayer time, Brandon's spiritual eyes opened, and he saw fire fall from Heaven and set everyone on fire. Then the scene shifted, and he saw what it would look like when we took the fire out into the world. As we began to speak to the people, fire would come out of our mouths and set the listeners on fire as well. Then the ones who were set on fire became the fire. Going out, they set even more people on fire. This chain-reaction that did not stop until the fire of God spread all over the Earth.

His vision is a perfect picture of who we are. Freely sharing Jesus from the place of love in Him will set the world on fire. The world doesn't want more religious philosophies, they are hungry for something real, something tangible, and something they can "put their hands" on and "sink their teeth into." They are hungry to experience the supernatural. It's not enough to just tell someone about God. Our words should be accompanied by fire. They don't need another sermon, they need an encounter with God.

My friend at the gym that day experienced a supernatural answer to his questions about evolution. His inquiry revealed that deep down he did not want to believe the evolution nonsense. Otherwise, he wouldn't have asked. He knew I loved God and needed someone to respond from God's perspective. He did not need an argument against the theory. He needed a demonstration that removed the theory.

A few years later, another fitness friend gave his life to Jesus, (through our friendship and others who were loving on him). One day, these two friends connected and had a conversation about God. The friend who had the encounter told the one who had recently been saved that he had never really believed in God until that day that God's presence showed up in the office. It was the first time in his life he felt the love of his heavenly Father. I knew God touched and changed his life that day, but I didn't realize just how significant it was until I heard this story.

FLAME-THROWERS

When Moses went to Pharaoh, he was now the bush that was burning. He did not just talk to Pharaoh about God. He demonstrated that he was sent by the "I AM WHO I AM." The Holy Spirit consumed the apostles as with Jesus. Because of this, they changed not only their own generation, but also every generation since. Can we not do the same? I have been baptized in the Holy Spirit over two decades, yet I know that there is more. I want to light up like the bush—on fire, but not burned up. There is more for all of us. I want to be a burning bush, a flame-thrower, a light to my generation and generations to come!

271

Only those who burn in the desert can impact the world. I want to burn like a bush, day and night so that when people get around me they take off their shoes of sin and sickness and discover his love. The fire came in the bush, the fire came in Jesus, and now the fire comes in us. We bring holiness with us. We are immersed in Holy Spirit's fire. We are burning bushes who walk the Earth. The all-encompassing heavenly realm is revealed through our lives. We are otherworldly. We have become one with the One who is the origin of the fire. We are the torches who light the world with the light of Jesus Christ.

ACTIVATION

If I have been successful, you've begun to burn for a greater baptism in the Holy Spirit. First, if you've never been baptized in the Spirit, now is the time. Second, if you haven't been in God's presence for some time, or you spoke in tongues once, today is the day for more. Third, even if you encounter the presence of God every single day, He always has more. Ask God to fill you with the fullness of His power and to take your further than you've ever been before.

Water baptism is a natural picture of Spirit baptism. You are drenched in the presence of the Holy Spirit from head to toe, inside to out. It's not just a special experience for some believers, but something that is available for all. God promised to pour out His Spirit on all flesh, including you.

The Baptism in the Holy Spirit isn't something you try to do; it's a gift you receive. Take a moment, either by yourself or with some friends, to find a place of rest where you are free of distractions. Invite Holy Spirit to fill you. Breathe in the experience. His presence manifests in many ways. You may feel a breeze, electricity, tingles, sounds, or other sensations. When God's presence comes, often there is a desire to express what is happening. It's as if something is welling up inside of you that needs to be let out. Simply add voice to what you're experiencing. As you do, you may find yourself speaking words you've never heard before. This is the language of Heaven.

In encounters like this, the mind can try to analyze the experience, which can lead to feeling like you're making it up. Allow the mind to rest while your spirit drinks in the presence of God.

Rest, invite, receive, and respond to God. I've seen many filled with the Spirit without responding, causing them to miss what God desired to give them. When Moses heard God's voice, he replied. There was an interaction. God showed up; then he drew near. When you ask God to show up, He will. When He does, draw near to Him, run to Him, and boldly express your heart to Him. Now is your time to release through your lips what is happening inside you. You may feel the fire of God burning in the depths of your being. God is filling you with Himself on the inside and covering with his presence on the outside. Don't rush. Stay in the encounter as long as you can.

This experience isn't just a one-time encounter. It's not a box to check. It's a lifestyle. We may know God is always with us, but we may not be aware of His presence. Keep the eyes of your spirit engaged with Him. Stay connected. You'll find that you can go through your whole day without leaving the encounter. Focus your mind on the excellence of your daily activities and interaction with people, but focus your spirit on sweet communion with God.

If you prayed in tongues for the first time, steward the gift. Pray in the Spirit whenever you get the chance. I pray in tongues multiple times a day. The gift is yours; you can activate it whenever you want. It will build up your inner man and invigorate your body. Tasks that take two hours will start to take one as you live your supernatural lifestyle.

From this day forward, each day is an invitation to more of God than yesterday. Keep going, keep burning, keep stirring yourself up in the fire of the Holy Spirit. Go higher, go deeper, go further, go wider!

In a journal, write out your encounter. As you write, you'll notice details you didn't realize you experienced. A million revelations can flash through one's mind in an encounter like this, so take the time to process and become everything you experienced in God.

DECLARATION

I will be a burning bush. I will be the encounter. I will demonstrate to the world of the power of God. I will live my life in God's presence. I will speak in heavenly languages. I will light up my life with the fire of God. I will light up the world!

RISE REVIVALIST!

THIRTEEN

DEPTHS OF GOD

**I LONG TO EXPLORE THE DEPTHS OF GOD JUST AS CAPTAIN KIRK EXPLORES SPACE···
TO BOLDLY GO WHERE NO ONE HAS GONE BEFORE!**

I grew up watching *Star Trek* with my dad. The voyages of Captain Kirk and his team to unknown worlds across the galaxy sparked a love for the cosmos in my imagination. "To boldly go where no man has gone before," was the last line of Kirk's prolog before each episode of the show. Each time I heard it, something inside of me would rise up. I wanted to go where no one has gone. I wanted to see and experience places that were unknown.

The idea of exploring the universe expanded when I caught a glimpse of the endless capacity of God. In fact, there is something at the core of the human race to go beyond the present and grab hold of the mystery. We were created to discover. Wonder activates the imagination. Imagination invites invention. Invention creates a vehicle for us to travel into the unknown. When we dream, it becomes the first step in launching out into our destinies.

Space is both immeasurable and incalculable. Think of its magnitude- spanning light years upon light years. Physicists try to decipher its secrets and unlock its hidden doors. Yet, our most powerful telescope is like looking through a keyhole into a stadium. However, the vastness of the cosmic realm hangs gently above the Earth, inviting us into its wonder.

EVEN THE DEPTHS

The universe is big: God is bigger... Imagine the universe—space in its ever-increasing-ness, all the galaxies, solar systems, and planets—sitting nicely in his hand. This illustration gives us a visualization for how big God truly is.

For the Spirit searches all things, even the depths of God.

1 Corinthians 2:10b NASB

Paul tells us here that the Spirit searches everything, including all that the universe contains, from the smallest atom to the biggest galaxy. The Spirit also has access to everything outside the universe—realms, and dimensions that are unfathomable. Not only does the Spirit search these things, but God Himself.

276

It is easy to picture the universe as a 3D box that has a region known as Heaven, which is where God lives. However, this is a limited perception of God. If God resides in the universe, then it leaves room for something or someone higher, which effectively—albeit unknowingly—disempowers both His grandeur and our relationship with Him. If we could see His reality, we would realize that He created the universe for us. His dimension is much bigger, all-encompassing, and all around us.

GOD DOESN'T **LIVE SOMEWHERE** IN THE **UNIVERSE:** THE **UNIVERSE LIVES SOMEWHERE** IN **GOD.**

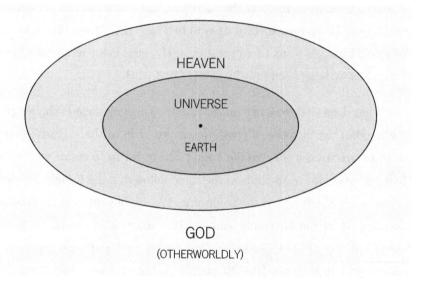

In the illustration, we see that all creation is included within God Himself—the realm of the otherworldly. Within Him is Heaven, within Heaven is the universe, within the universe is the Earth. Often, we take a reverse look at this and lose the enormity of God. He spoke and created the heavens and the Earth, "the universe and all it contains." "All things are from Him, through Him, and to Him." "Everything was made through Him, and apart from Him, nothing was made that has been made." Heaven is the setting for Earth, and God is the setting for Heaven.

Star Trek gives a creative picture of what it could be like to travel from planet to planet and galaxy to galaxy. If the entirety of the universe fits into the hand of God, then we are granted a new perspective on everything we thought we knew. The exploration of space is one thing, the exploration of God is another. Imagine exploring God the same way as a spaceship sails through the heavens, flying from this place to place inside His heart. If we were the crew, think of the discoveries out there to be made, how awesome His thoughts are, and "what is the surpassing greatness of His power toward us who believe," (Eph 1:19). Through the Spirit, God reveals to us these mysteries. His goal is for us to fully know him just as we have been fully known (1 Cor 13:12).

What does God look like on the inside? This language is challenging to some, but the purpose of creation was for Him to share Himself with us. Jesus prepared a place in the Father's heart for us to reside with Him. He made a way for us to abide in the same fellowship the Father, the Son, and the Holy Spirit had in the beginning. We are in God, and He is in us. We are part of the Heavenly Family. This marvelous revelation is the essence of the Gospel. Knowing God inside and out will generate a witness that introduces Him to people inside and out. When we live inside the heart of God, we can recreate His heart in the Earth. We are like great explorers who share their treasures for all the world to see.

MYRIAD

And, just how big is God? Saying He is bigger than the universe almost loses touch with reality. Let's take a mathematical approach. The enormity and vastness of God are indeed beyond calculation, but giving illustrations helps us find a place to connect.

The Bible often uses the term myriad to describe something on a too expansive to quantify, like the waves of the sea or a swarm of insects. Myriad is ten thousand. It was uncountable, but comprehensible.

If you could zoom-in, and had the patience, you would discover there are 10,000, or a myriad of dots in the image. You can see it, but counting it would be daunting.

In Revelation 5:11, John says there are ten thousand times ten thousand angels encircling God's throne, or a myriad of myriads. 10,000 x's 10,000 represented something that was both uncountable and incomprehensible. John used imagery rather than precision to show there was an infinite number of them. His articulation grants us a snapshot of the heavenly realm and reveals that everything happens there is on a much bigger plane than it happens on the Earth. John's choice of language created a construct for enormity and superiority of existence he witnessed.

GOOGOL

If we fast-forward to our time, myriad is used more to create a sense of wonder and majesty. It invokes the feeling of enormity and is more of an idea than a technicality. However, we live in a technological age where larger numerical equations are processed billions of times in a single day. We may not be able to count it ourselves, but we've built computers that can. Tech requires a new grid of consideration. What a *myriad* was in biblical times, a *googol* is in modern times.

A *googol* is a number that has 100 zeros after it. A googolplex is a number that has a googol zeros after it. No, they are not the same thing. Take a look at the googol below:

- A **googol** is the large number 10^{100}, that is, the digit 1 followed by one hundred zeros:

  10,000,000,000,000,000,000,000,000,000,000,
  000,000,000,000,000,000,000,000,000,000,
  000,000,000,000,000,000,000,000,000,000

Many of us have great visions of how big God is, but we may just be looking at Him as a googol. When we arrive at capacity to comprehend Him in a *googolplex*, we will see him on a massively larger scale.

- A **googolplex** is the number 10^{googol}, i.e. $10^{10^{100}}$, also written as the number 1 followed by googol zeros (i.e., 10^{100} zeros).

GOOGOLPLEX

10,000,000,000,000,000,000,000,000,000,000,000,000,000,000,00
0,000,000,000,000,000,000,000,000,000,000,000,000,000,000,000
,000,000,000,000,000,000,000,000,000,000,000,000,000,000,000,
000,000,000,000,000,000,000,000,000,000,000,000,000,000,000,0
00,000,000,000,000,000,000,000,000,000,000,000,000,000,000,00
0,000,000,000,000,000,000,000,000,000,000,000,000,000,000,000
,000,000,000,000,000,000,000,000,000,000,000,000,000,000,000,
000,000,000,000,000,000,000,000,000,000,000,000,000,000,000,0
00,000,000,000,000,000,000,000,000,000,000,000,000,000,000,00
0,000,000,000,000,000,000,000,000,000,000,000,000,000,000,000
,000,000,000,000,000,000,000,000,000,000,000,000,000,000,000,
000,000,000,000,000,000,000,000,000,000,000,000,000,000,000,0
00,000,000,000,000,000,000,000,000,000,000,000,000,000,000,00
0,000,000,000,000,000,000,000,000,000,000,000,000,000,000,000
,000,000,000,000,000,000,000,000,000,000,000,000,000,000,000,
000,000,000,000,000,000,000,000,000,000,000,000,000,000,000,0
00,000,000,000,000,000,000,000,000,000,000,000,000,000,000,00
0,000,000,000,000,000,000,000,000,000,000,000,000,000,000,000
,000,000,000,000,000,000,000,000,000,000,000,000,000,000,000,
000,000,000,000,000,000,000,000,000,000,000,000,000,000,000,0
00,000,000,000,000,000,000,000,000,000,000,000,000,000,000,00 etc.

There are approximately 1083 zeros above. Pretty big huh? Now let's try to capture this. One million is a number with six zeros behind it. So, if we call a number a "millionplex," it would be a number with a million zeros behind it. There are only 1083 zeros above, which is 998,917 short of a million. If I were to type out 1,000,000 zeros, you would be able to see what a "millionplex" looks like written out. It will fill more than this entire book with just zeroes. To arrive at the sum, a "millionplex" represents we would have 100's of libraries filled with 100's of millions of books full of zeroes. The next level is the googol. To get there, we would have hundreds of millions of libraries each filled with 100's of millions of books with only zeroes in them. That is just to write it in long form. The illustrate the sum it represents; we would have hundreds of trillions of earths, all filled with 100's of millions of libraries filled with 100's of millions of books with only zeroes in them. As for the googolplex... "Well, that escalated quickly!"

Okay, let's look at it from another angle. A googol has 100 zeros after it, not just six as we see in 1,000,000. A googolplex would have the sum of the googol in zeros after "1". Just as a millionplex would have a million zeros, a googolplex would have a googol zeros. The sum is so great that universe doesn't contain a total number of hydrogen atoms that could equal a googol! What? That is unimaginable! We aren't done yet, however. If you were to fill up the universe in its entirety with microscopic dots, you would not even come close to having a googolplex in zeros.

Million	1,000,000	6 Zeros
Googol	10^{100}	100 Zeros
Millionplex	$10^{1000000}$	1,000,000 Zeros
Googolplex	$10^{10(100)}$	10^{100} Zeros

Think of this table as multidimensional. Each layer is incalculably bigger than the previous one. The Million level represents our world and all that we are able to comprehend. The Googol would be the entirety of the universe. The Millionplex is the heavenly realm. As for the Googolplex, this could represent the realm of God Himself.

THE BEYOND

Space is the googol, and God is the googolplex. And that is just an illustration that I can fathom with my mind. He is far above and beyond all that we can ask or think. If humans can dream up the number, googolplex, just imagine the mind of God. Googolplex isn't even the most substantial number. It gets crazy with operational levels and power towers, which are tools used just to arrive a sum known as Graham's Number. These calculations are done to measure dimensions in a hypercube. Now we are getting trans-dimensional and multi-universal There's a grander number even still, known as "TREE(3)." I won't attempt to describe it, but you can search for it on Google.

Technology and the human mind today are scratching the surface with something John experienced 2000 years ago.

AS **HEAVEN** AND **EARTH REUNITE**, THE **KNOWLEDGE** OF **GOD RISES**.

Mysteries revealed restore creation to the image of God. The increase of sons and daughters who think transformatively will exponentially innovate, accelerate, and sky-rocket technological advancement. The Apostle Paul had similar encounters that were so staggering; he was unable to articulate the experience:

> "I will go on to visions and revelations of the Lord. I know a man in Christ who fourteen years ago was caught up to the third heaven—whether in the body or out of the body I do not know, God knows. And I know that this man was caught up into paradise—whether in the body or out of the body I do not know, God knows—and he heard things that cannot be told, which man may not utter.

> 2 Corinthians 12:1a-4

Again, one of the faults of is to think of God in terms of the universe. The universe came from His breath. His majesty and infinite power would require language we are unable to speak. To translate His world to ours, His Son became like us and walked among us. He didn't travel from "Planet Heaven" at the far end of the universe to arrive on Earth.

HE HUMBLED HIMSELF TO **PHASE** INTO THIS **REALM**, SO **HE** COULD **SHOW US** HOW TO **PHASE** INTO **HIS REALM.**

He invites us into Himself, into the beyond. Earth exist in the heavenly realm, and the heavenly realm exists in God Himself. The entirety of the cosmos was in Him on the Earth. And through Him, we have access to all of the cosmos, all of Heaven, and all of God.

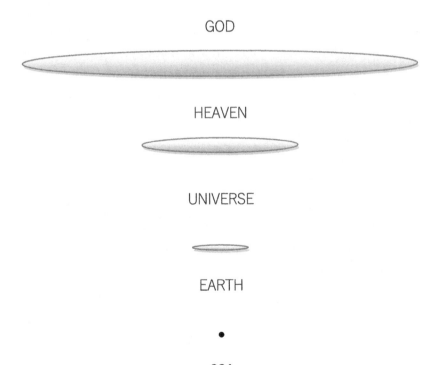

GOD

HEAVEN

UNIVERSE

EARTH

•

John and Paul both made the trip through the realms of existence from earth to heaven. John stood on the sea of glass and saw the splendor of God standing on His throne. He saw the Eternal Family. The earthly man in him trembled as the heavenly man became more alive than ever. To stand in the presence of the engine that fires the universe and observe the command center for all that exists transcends reality. To arrive in Heaven isn't just a physical ascension, it's also a spiritual ascension. With every glance, every thought, every sound, John transformed. He discovered the purpose of his animation, his reason for being, and destiny in life. Just appearing there caused John to begin to think and calculate like Heaven. The external became his internal, and when he returned to Earth, his internal began to reprogram his external.

We will never understand the information in Revelation unless we commune in the experience. One cannot apprehend Heaven from Earth. You have to go to Heaven to apprehend Heaven. "Unless one is born from above he cannot see the Kingdom of Heaven," (John3). Many experts of spirituality have never actually been to heavenly places. Believing it exist and living life there are two totally different things. Just because someone's heavenly residence counteracts earthly paradigms, it doesn't make them a heretic. I tend to believe the ones who've seen the perspective of the Author when deciding the authenticity of biblical theology. The Book of Revelation reveals Heaven's view of events happening on Earth. This paradigm isn't limited to Westernized thought or time. You'll only comprehend it—as with all Scripture—if you are seated in heavenly places, observing life through the lenses of the Spirit. John architected what he saw in Heaven on the Earth. This is the purpose and design of encounter.

Paul is less descriptive: Either he, after 14 years, was still unable to share in any earthly language the details of his encounter, or he saw things that remain hidden from the Earth—although he was granted early access. Nonetheless, now we know how he was able to so masterfully write about heavenly places in Ephesians. Both men transformed the planet through the frameworks given to them in heavenly places. The location to such glorious encounters is in the secret place of intimacy. Being in love with Jesus is access to everything God has to offer.

CENTRIFUGAL EXPONENTIAL REVELATION

Isn't it amazing that advances in mathematics can give insight into the lives of John and Paul, and the relationship between Heaven and Earth? What if we were able to see on par with the mathematics of God. Imagine thinking on His level. Let's look at the creation of the universe through this lens: "Let there be light," is the center, "1". Once spoken, "nothing" began to be populated by creation. Centrifugal means moving out from the center, "1". The digit "1" is the center, then as you add, multiply, and exponentially raise it from the center, you have an ever-expanding revelation—continuously adding revelation to revelation. This is kind of like the math tools I mentioned earlier such as observational levels and power towers; there are even hypercubes and trees. Each plane is a is much more expansive than the previous. New numbers in math emerge in quantifying the next plane, not just adding or multiplying.

I've tried to explain it, now let's try to experience it. Picture God saying, "Let there be light." His voice thunders as creation erupts from His very being. The sound comes alive as vibrating waves of light. This light, born in the depths of God—who is the Light—begins to shape reality, from the smallest bit of string theory, spiraling upward and outward, rapidly filling the universe in all directions.

The radical part is that God is both centrifugal and centripetal. He created everything that is seen and known from within Himself in a way that is seemingly forever expanding. And at the same time, He is drawing all things to Himself. He both sends us out and calls us in. Many refer to this as the "Divine Dance."

IN OUR EXPLORATIONS, THE FURTHEST WE MAY GO IN OUR ADVENTURE WILL FIND US RIGHT IN THE MIDDLE OF HIS HEART.

Centrifugal perception of God also reveals how we grow as believers. He created all that we see and know, and daily reveals more of Himself to us. In the New Testament, the writers and apostles pray and encourage us to have revelation to comprehend God's love, power, riches, etc. To summarize it, His love and thoughts and ways are infinite. They are eternal and ever increasing as we go and grow. He is forever—from forever past, to forever forward. These numbers are an example of our utter inability to measure God on any human scale, yet give us a framework for our exploration.

I believe this helps us capture the essence of that which Paul describes in the 2nd chapter of 1st Corinthians. Through the Holy Spirit, we have the capacity to comprehend such things, even the depths of God. The wisdom of God is incomprehensible without the Spirit and the knowledge of God.

I am having trouble describing a simple number to you. Now imagine all that is involved in the Father, the Son, and the Holy Spirit.

For to us God revealed *them* through the Spirit; for the Spirit searches all things, even the depths of God. For who among men knows the *thoughts* of a man except the spirit of the man which is in him? Even so the *thoughts* of God no one knows except the Spirit of God. Now we have received, not the spirit of the world, but the Spirit who is from God, so that we may know the things freely given to us by God, which things we also speak, not in words taught by human wisdom, but in those taught by the Spirit, combining spiritual *thoughts* with spiritual *words*.

But a natural man does not accept the things of the Spirit of God, for they are foolishness to him; and he cannot understand them, because they are spiritually appraised. But he who is spiritual appraises all things, yet he himself is appraised by no one. For WHO HAS KNOWN THE MIND OF THE LORD, THAT HE WILL INSTRUCT HIM? But we have the mind of Christ.

1 Corinthians 2:10-16 NASB

All that we have described up to this point makes us thinking like God seem impossible. Does it not say, however, that what is impossible with man is possible with God? Now we realized what it means when it was said, "Who may know the mind of the Lord, that he will instruct Him? Ah, but wait, here comes the secret. We can think like God because we have the same Spirit as God. Therefore, we have the mind of Christ. God's mind could engulf the universe an unlimited number of times. This is the place the Spirit searches and reveals to us the secrets found there. What an astronomical image!

The wise men in Pharaoh's court were probably the wisest in the world at that time. They were the googols. Then Moses appears with the power of "I am." He was the "Centrifugal Exponential Revelation." They had power, but the power Moses possessed wasn't simply more powerful, it registered on a completely different scale. The same goes for us. "We are seated with Him in heavenly places," which is far above all rule and authority and power and dominion, and every name that is named, not only in this age but also in the one to come," (Eph 1:21; 2:6).

APOSTOLIC GALAXY

To be apostolic is to live from this place of the Spirit revealing to us the depths of God. Revelation that is sent from God to create a culture of Heaven on Earth is the function of the apostolic church.

One thing that I have come to realize is that in the exploration of a galaxy, the understanding of a planet is necessary for the understanding of the galaxy. However, the planet alone does not describe the galaxy. The micro and the macro are both needed for the complete picture. The digit "1" is the key to the myriad. God desires to explore our hearts the same way He invites us to explore His. When we unite as Family, the fellowship of revelations comes together, and a picture will be painted for the next generation to follow and believe. I hope to encounter other explorers of this apostolic galaxy, ones who have visited planets I have yet to hear of and show me things I have yet to see. Faith is a vast exploration, the validation of life and existence. There is more of God every second of every day. Consider the sand and the stars, countless as they are, they are not but one breath, one thought of His majestic glory. O' that we may see and gain wisdom into His majesty. All life comes from Him. The exploration of Him is far grander than that of galaxies and His gifts to us are majestic.

Just imagine what can happen within the possibilities of God, where the furthest, most unfathomable idea slides right underneath our feet like a galactic surfboard, taking us from planet to planet in the myriad of His being. Let us surf the waves flowing from God's heart. They reveal the apostolic revelation for us to take hold of our times and emerge as revivalists. God's heart is larger than worlds and vaster than oceans. If we traced the expanse of the universe and all the beauty thereof, it would not even touch the infinite pleasure of the hem of His garment.

SPACE ENCOUNTERS

I have had several encounters both on the galactic level and on the heavenly level, which are often hard to differentiate. Once, during a prayer meeting, I was sitting in my chair thinking about the cosmic majesty of God when, all of the sudden, I found myself flying around a galaxy faster than the speed of light. I could see the brightly lit center and all the stars spiraling out from it. I realized that while my physical body was at the prayer meeting, my spirit had traveled to some distant galaxy.

It was so intense that I was unable to remain in the encounter for more than a few seconds before I found myself back in the chair. Once back on Earth, I wanted to see and experience more. In the next moment, I was back at the galaxy. I was able to endure a few moments longer this time around before it became too much. Again, I was back in my chair with the prayer meeting happening around me. The motion of flying around the galaxy was so intense that it felt like I was trying to hang on to the back of a speeding roller coaster.

When we are used to functioning in an earthly atmosphere, it takes determination, endurance, adaptation to experience heavenly atmospheres. This reaction is evident in both Ezekiel and John's language when they described their otherworldly experiences. I went back and forth several times in the encounter over a period of about five minutes.

This experience came after I heard a testimony from someone who had galactic encounters. Just as I view encounters in the Bible as invitations into my encounters, I do the same with ones I hear today that resonate with my heart and Holy Spirit within me.

THE FACE OF JESUS

Another experience I had like this was enriched with a direct encounter with the face of Jesus, although, I didn't know it at first. I had the encounter many times over the years, each offering greater depth. Initially, I found myself staring at a cluster of galaxies. I could see stars and planets, and other heavenly bodies. As I began to scan the scene, I found I was looking at an iris made of the cosmos. This encounter was intense as well because it was so majestic and beautiful, I felt as if I would melt into it. Over time, I would go back into the encounter and see new pieces of the puzzle. One day, after repeatedly trying to go into the eye, I zoomed out... And found myself staring into the face of Jesus. A whole new world opened before me. The face of Jesus was there the whole time, but it was only revealed after activating the encounter numerous times to experience more and discover what God hid for me in the mystery.

ACTIVATION

The heavenly encounters I've had are vast, some of which I described earlier in the book. I am grateful to have had them, but I am not a special recipient of encounters. God has created all of us to encounter Him. I share my experiences as an invitation for you activate encounters of your own. Heaven is waiting for you to come and see so that you can go and reproduce.

Find a place where you won't be interrupted so you can disengage the earthly realm and engage the heavenly realm. Ask Jesus to come and be with you. Tell Him you want to experience the wonder of creation. Ask Holy Spirit to guide you into the depths of God. Wait until you are through to write out the experience. His voice is but one aspect of the encounter. Go deeper into a multi-sensory encounter. What do you see, hear, feel, taste, smell, and experience? Throw yourself fully into the heavenly places prepared for you. Father is a safe place for you to unlock and activate your supernatural lifestyle.

SEE

HEAR

FEEL

TASTE

SMELL

EXPERIENCE

DECLARATION

I am created for encounters. I have the mind of Christ and access to the depths of God. I will become a heavenly doorway for those in my life to experience the treasures, love, and power Jesus has for them.

RISE REVIVALIST!

FOURTEEN

EYES OF IMAGINATION

GOD IS LIMITLESS AND INFINITE.

I enjoy travel shows. The exotic locations inspire me. I often use pictures that capture a majestic mountaintop, misty castle, or a long exposure of the Milky Way as background images. They allow me to enjoy the beauty of this world. I dream of visiting these breathtaking locations and imagine what it's like to be there. External stimulus drives me to see through the eyes of my imagination. A tropical beach is an invitation for me to feel its sand beneath my feet and its water splash over me. My sight inspires me to imagine the experience. My imagination is a catalyst to create a plan to travel to its shores.

TV, books, and movies transport us to places we visualized in imagination. We are inspired to do more, to be brave and launch out into our destinies... Yet, how often does it get push back until "next year"? We may have a subconscious block that prevents us from taking a step into what we imagine today. We must find a way past our minds to a place where our dreams begin to take shape, to a place where we pull the future into the present.

Testimonies are external stimuli for us to experience God in the way the one testifying has experienced Him. If they received healing, we are inspired to receive our healing, or to heal others. If encounters, like the one I described in the last chapter, then we are motivated to encounter God as they did. If it's a Bible story, then we are inspired to experience God as they did in the Bible.

Just as seeing an ad for a vacation, when I hear of someone else's God encounter, I imagine what it would be like to "go there" too. If my friend visits the beach I've seen on TV and describes it to me, then I have a firsthand account of what it is actually like. This book is my account of what living a supernatural lifestyle is like and an invitation for you to join me.

LIMITLESS

God is limitless and infinite. He is One who is Three and Three who are One. We see in part because He is available to be known in so many different ways. Heaven is a reflection of who He is. Everything about Him sparks the imagination. Exposure to His goodness draws us to Him. We want to know the depths of his being. Jesus came to testify about what God is really like. His life demonstrated it. His story is an invitation to "go there too." He is the "Way" to experience and encounter God.

Several years ago, while in a dialog with a friend, I made the statement that "Christian theology often limits a limitless God." His response was challenging, "Christian theology limiting a limitless God is what caused me to entirely reject Christian theology." My friend is a dreamer, ahead of his time, and the "Christian Box" had no room for his ideas. Asking questions and viewing things, especially doctrines, from different angles, doesn't' usually feel safe to those who have found their identity in what they believe, rather than as sons and daughters of God. Often, it will result in rejecting, or worse, demonizing those who think differently. I do not think my friend has rejected Jesus, quite the contrary, but I can see how it is hard to relate to a theology absent of imagination, which declares "our God is not a Dreamer."

Western Christianity places more emphasis on knowing the truth, rather than feeling the truth. The head trumps the heart even if the heart cries danger. Dreamers are not managed like thinkers. Both are needed, but our society promotes one and misunderstands the other. Learning to dream will ignite the imagination to think in a heavenly way.

The conversation with my friend stemmed from a post I made on Facebook: "So often we see God as a solo act when He is a symphony in and of Himself." There are many layers to God, but we may only see Him through the present layer. Remember, God is so big that He runs all the endless probable universes and so focused that He loves each one of us dearly—concerned about even the smallest details of our lives—knowing the number of hairs on our heads.

Our worldview will determine the layer we are viewing Him through. As I am sure you have heard before; "The forest is not the tree, and the tree is not the forest." Lifting our vision higher and seeing just how deep, awesome and big our God is will allow us to imagine and dream on new levels, upgrading both the small details and the big picture.

MANY LAYERS OF GOD

> And to bring to light for everyone what is the plan of the mystery hidden for ages in God who created all things, so that through the church the manifold wisdom of God might now be made known to the rulers and authorities in the heavenly places. This was according to the eternal purpose that he has realized in Christ Jesus our Lord.

> Ephesians 3:9-11 ESV

Here, I want to take a closer look at the word "manifold" and its meaning.

> *polypoíkilos* (an adjective, derived from *polýs*, "much in number, many" and *poikílos*, "many diverse manifestations") — properly, ultra-diverse, with multitudinous expressions (facets).[1]

Whoa, let's plug that into the verse: "'Many diverse manifestations' of the wisdom of God." If you think understanding the human mind is complex, just fathom the mind of God. Remember, the secret is that "we have the mind of Christ," accessing the deepest parts of God. He has given us the mind to think like Him, imagine like Him, and dream like Him.

Our imagination opens up a whole new world for us. If we read the Bible and imagine being with Jesus as a disciple, then it creates an attachment point for us experience Him in the same, yet uniquely personal way. Imagination—seeing with the eyes of our spirit—constructs possibility and expectancy within us.

IMAGINING WHAT GOD CAN DO LEADS TO THE RUNWAY OF "WHAT GOD IS DOING."

He takes pleasure in us dreaming about Him. It's a circle of life. He gives us an imagination as a place for awe and wonder to develop so we can have the capacity to believe for Him to do impossible things in our lives.

Thinking this way is thinking from above. A famous Albert Einstein quote reveals the how imagination enhances knowledge:

"IMAGINATION IS MORE IMPORTANT THAN KNOWLEDGE. KNOWLEDGE IS LIMITED. IMAGINATION ENCIRCLES THE WORLD."

The design of the spiritual life is of one that knows no boundaries between Heaven and Earth, natural and supernatural. We see this perfected in the life of Jesus. He modeled it for us because it is the true intention of how we are supposed to live. Imagination takes flight when the supernatural is natural. We are a new creation—heavenly beings of flesh and blood, and spirit and fire.

To activate our imagination, it is elemental that we remain childlike. Reason will cloud dreams with the stormy weather of "playing it safe." The imagination of a child is clear as a sunny day, daring to take flight from the smallest stump left for leaping.

Imagination is so powerful because what happens on the inside of us begins to happen around us. When Heaven is constructed in us, then it will begin to manifest around us. Verses that inspire us become leaping stumps from which to fly.

When our spiritual eyes see where we really are, then our physical eyes will gain sight beyond the natural realm. We are far too familiar with our natural existence while being unfamiliar with our heavenly placement.

Ephesians is a roadmap to realizing that we are seated in heavenly places and how we function there.

> Blessed be the God and Father of our Lord Jesus Christ, who has blessed us with every spiritual blessing in the heavenly places in Christ.
>
> vv 1-3 NASB

Where are we blessed? *In heavenly places.* What are we blessed with? *Every spiritual blessing.*

> Which he brought about in Christ, when He raised Him from the dead and seated Him at His right hand in the heavenly places, far above all rule and authority and power and dominion, and every name that is named, not only in this age but also in the one to come.
>
> vv 1:20-21

Where is Jesus seated? He is at the highest attainable place in existence, at the right hand of the Father—equal to the highest height. Who is above him in dominion and authority? No one, nothing; He is above them all, both in this age (earthly) and the one to come (heavenly). No name is above His.

> And raised us up with Him, and seated us with Him in
> the heavenly places in Christ Jesus.

> v 2:6

Where are we seated? At his right hand in heavenly places. How many heavenly authorities are above us? None. What is above us? Nothing. We are members of the Family, above which nothing exists. This is our place in the heavenly realm. According to the text, we are at the highest obtainable rank in time and eternity, while living on Earth. God the Father, Jesus the Son, and Holy Spirit are above us within the Family, yet they placed us at the right hand of the Right Hand. We abide in the plane of Family. We now have God's view of the world, of time, and of everything else. We get to think like Him because He sat us right next to Him. If we can comprehend this, then we will experience true transformation.

Just a few passages later in Ephesians 3, Paul describes the comprehension of God's love in this manner:

> You may be able to comprehend with all the saints what
> is the breadth and length and height and depth.

> v 18 NASB

I might be stretching it, but I feel like Paul uses four measurements to illustrate a four-dimensional view of the love of God. I think the fourth dimension is the supernatural realm. This dimension is where we truly live. When we activate our residence here, we become like Jesus. As the barrier between Heaven and Earth fades, we will see things as they are.

FAITH SENSORY PERCEPTION

Faith is the manifesto to see the unseen. Prophetic imagination opens the eyes of the spirit man. In the natural, sight is a sense that constructs the world around us to guide us in our animation. Likewise, faith constructs the heavenly world to guide us in our animation there. Sight is a stream of data telling our brain how to navigate natural life. Faith is a stream of data telling our spirit how to navigate the spiritual life. These two streams are either often left separated by belief systems or neglected altogether, except for "seers." The sense of sight and the spiritual sense of faith can become one. I believe in the gift of seer, but I also believe that God desires all of us to see and function in this world. The way we "see" as Family will become otherworldly. "Seated in heavenly places" isn't just a neat idea, it's an actual place to function and exist. The famous "Faith" passage in Hebrews accentuates this point:

> Now faith is the substance of things hoped for, the evidence of things not seen.

> v 11:1 KJV

Faith proves that what we do not see exists. When we believe, we see with a different kind of sight. Believing is seeing. What we see there will become a reality here. If we see the mountain move, we will experience the shift.

Intimacy in Family cultivates spiritual sight. Being with them is an experience in their interaction and dynamic as Family. Contained within the union of the heavenly Family is an environment without limits. Every impossible thing is realized, which is why Family is so powerful. It enforces original design. Sin, sickness, and death cannot exist here. Amazingly, when we live here, sin, sickness, and death cannot exist in us either. As we function in Family, we create communities who nurture this kind of existence. Society will take notice and cultures will become the culture of the Family of God.

When our prophetic imagination is activated, it will also enhance our other senses. That which we've experienced in dreams and visions will begin to bleed into our daily lives. We will start to see with our spirit and with our eyes simultaneously. As children of God, we will see with our Father's worldview. Our sense of sight, sound, smell, taste, and touch will all be upgraded to a heavenly mode of operation. Identifying our place in the Family will bring a supernatural enhancement to our daily lives.

THE VERANDA VISION

One afternoon, while lying down to take a nap, I was interrupted by a vision. I was in the in-between state of being awake and asleep. All of the sudden, I saw into the spiritual realm with my natural eyes. My physical surroundings were pulled back like curtains drawn on a stage. The veil itself was composed of natural matter- my bed, the wall, and all that I could see. These elements did not lose their shape or structure as they moved apart to reveal the realm beyond the veil. The natural was the curtain to the supernatural. It was always there, but now it was visible.

I began to animate with a heavenly encounter, even-though my body lay still on my bed. I walked through the opening out onto a veranda. It was Romanesque in appearance, white with Corinthian columns, which were about waist high. They seemed to be some type of pedestal. The veranda had a round shape on the west-facing side, which overlooked a gentle slope below. As I surveyed the landscape, it seemed as if we were on the side of a mountain overlooking the Earth. It was lush and green with vineyards. It wasn't like a Google satellite photo. Instead, it looked much different and contained elements that seemed to indicate spiritual climates across the plane. Lines of trees connected as if they were the highways. Clearly, there is a lot hidden here as God sees how we are connected much differently than we see. It reminded me of "God's path through the city," yet it was His path across the Earth.

The whole setting had an ancient feel. It was old—very old—yet technologically beyond anything I had ever experienced. At the time I had this encounter, I had been listening to techno artist, Phutureprimitive (future-primitive). This name weirdly described the impression of this place. It felt as simple as a primitive way of life a thousand years ago, yet as futuristic as a thousand years from now. Often, the thought of advanced tech dials up the idea of all kinds of gadgets and gizmos. However, this vision exceeded that way of thinking. There was perfect peace. It wasn't hectic or chaotic; instead, it was elementary in its stillness. This level of futurism can only emerge from the simplicity that comes from a primitive mindset. Papa Leif describes this as "going back to the future."

IF WE SEE GOD AS HE IS IN THE BEGINNING, THEN WE WILL SEE HIM AS HE IS IN THE END— ALPHA AND OMEGA.

Standing in the center of the veranda was a lady dressed in an appearance that was Romanesque as well. She was wearing a white toga draped over one shoulder. A small golden cord fastened around her waist. Her skin was light, and her hair was a deep black. She carried such authority that it was easy to concede that this was her veranda. Total rest reigned over her countenance as she overlooked the Earth. She was more alive than any human I had ever met. In her rest, she was active, ruling over her sphere of influence in the earth from this heavenly place. Her demeanor was the source of the peace I felt earlier. She was alive with unhindered cosmic harmony. I first thought that she must be an angel. Then I considered that she was one of the cloud of witnesses because of her white garments. It wasn't until I revisited the encounter later that I realized she was a person living on the Earth in my generation. I went beyond the veil to witness someone from earth ruling and reigning in her heavenly place.

"Reigning in life" is a theme Leif uses to describe living life in alignment with Papa God. From this alignment flows our assignment. This lady wasn't doing much outwardly, but she was fully engaged in her assignment. So much was happening that it was hard to comprehend. The level of sophistication related to the function of her assignment was above any attempt to ascertain, yet she remained at total rest. More than that, the more she rested, the more she accomplished. Responsibility infused with purpose, which created the ability to relax because she was born for this. I then realized that her veranda was one of the control rooms that governed the mainframe of the Earth.

As she flowed in her gifts, there were flashes above the Roman columns that looked like holograms. They were projections from the earthly realm. It was a flip-flop. In the earthly, we have visions—flashes of the heavenly world in the natural world. Here, there were flashes of the earthly world in the heavenly world. The columns anchored what was happening on the Earth to a heavenly place. The lady reigned over this area of life and secured the scene to the projection portrayed in the cosmos. This moment was special for me because it revealed a 3D model of the reality that Heaven is the setting for the Earth. I believed this to be true before, but now I've seen and experienced it from the other side.

Faith invites encounters. Through faith, I find the restful invitation to experience a heavenly reality. I literally became one of the holograms from the Earth discovering where I am grounded in heavenly places. It was in resting in the natural—taking a nap—that I discovered how one reigns in Heaven.

Above the veranda, there were other fragments of light floating around. As the lady reigned in the area associated with the light, the light also grounded into one of the columns. The lights represented everything from people, to places, businesses, nations, ways of thinking, and so on. She transformed the Earth from her seat of rest and authority. The natural parts of creation that were governed by chaos—out there floating around with no connection—were synced through cosmos to their divine intention. They reconnected to Family through the lady in her seat of government in the ecclesia.

In the big picture, Heaven is the setting for the Earth. Some places on Earth were connected, some were not, but all the Earth was in Heaven's setting. All creation groans to belong, to be connected, to be part of the Family. As sons and daughters rise, Family is revealed, chaos is dethroned, and God's will is perfected. Finding your place in the Family grounds you in heavenly places. Where Family manifests, Father, Son, and Spirit manifest. Then, the reason for creation is united with its purpose.

The lady was aware of all the wonders happening around us, but wasn't doing any outward activity. She was almost subconsciously interacting with each scene from the earth. The peace that permeated her being would project onto the light fragment, and like lightning, it would ground into heaven. She was ruling through peace. Over-and-over again the separations were removed as they went from chaos to cosmos. These transformations reveal the cosmic structure that is in place. Earth is the hologram and Heaven is the construct. Each time we have a heavenly vision or encounter, Heaven's rule establishes on the Earth. Heaven is the setting for Earth, but Holy Spirit chooses to reside on the Earth in us—sons and daughters.

Since the Veranda Vision, I've had eyes to see the "Matrix." Not in a way that over-spiritualizes everything, but in a way that sees how the Earth is set in Heaven. Heaven's influence and design are evident. Now I can interact with the desire of God's heart for everything and everyone to realize their place in the Family. The testimony of this vision is an invitation for you to discover your heavenly place. It will probably look entirely different than the lady's because it is designed for you. Now you know it is available. Faith is the substance of things hoped for...and the evidence of things unseen...

TRANSFORMING THE MIND

When we begin to see things through the eyes of our spirit and from our seat in heavenly places, we will begin to think like God. This paradigm is a transformation of the mind. The term in Scripture is metanoia. It means to "trans-think," or think again on a higher level.

In the New Testament, metanoia most often translates as "repentance." However, the idea has nothing to do with the traditional Western Evangelical understanding. Repent, or repentance is often mistaken for meaning to feel sorry for your sins, or to turn from your sins. The direct translation of repentance in both Latin and Greek etymologies is "the payment of money to get rid of pollution [poena]," or "to repay blood money [poine]." Because of this, much of the church understands repentance this way. Many are stuck in endless cycles of sin and repentance because they are trying to subconsciously pay for their sins through the "act" of repentance, rather than the finished work of Jesus on the cross. There is the idea of repentance in the OT and NT—the concept of coming to God and turning from sin, which is essential and valid—but, it fails to capture the fullness of metanoia and the value intended. If we begin to think according to the payment Jesus made, it will remove the desire to repay. We've been repaying when we should be rethinking. "You're thinking like an earthling. Now is the time to think like a heavenly being." Changing how we think will change how we live. I'm not de-emphasizing the traditional view of repentance; rather, I am expanding to so include so much more. A mind that sees what Heaven

308

sees will begin to live life it is in Heaven. Life in the Earth lived like life in Heaven will reproduce heavenly life in those who encompass it. The lady in the vision had the mind of Christ; therefore, she was able to change thought patterns in the Earth.

Now we will plug our new definition of repentance into a verse:

> From that time Jesus began to preach and say, "Repent, for the kingdom of heaven is at hand."
>
> Matthew 4:17 NASB

The verse could also transliterate as: "Change the way that you think, the Kingdom of Heaven has drawn near." Now in mentioning Kingdom, there is a knowledge that accompanies it. All that the Law and the Prophets spoke of and prophesied of is now fulfilled because the heavenly Kingdom described by them has come. This fulfillment is something that only the Messiah could accomplish. Jesus is the Kingdom in Himself. To capture this requires a massive shift in thinking. This Kingdom is the one referenced earlier in Daniel 2. It is the city being built by God in the Earth. Only those who think this way and live a lifestyle of Heaven's thoughts can apprehend it.

> For those who are according to the flesh set their minds on the things of the flesh, but those who are according to the Spirit, the things of the Spirit. For the mind set on the flesh is death, but the mind set on the Spirit is life and peace...
>
> Romans 8:5, 6 NASB

We now think according to the Spirit, with transformed minds. The new mind hasn't exchanged an old set of rules for a new set of rules, but exchanged fleshly desires for heavenly desires.

> Therefore I urge you, brethren, by the mercies of God, to present your bodies a living and holy sacrifice, acceptable to God, which is your spiritual service of worship. And do not be conformed to this world, but be transformed by the renewing of your
>
> mind, so that you may prove what the will of God is, that which is good and acceptable and perfect.
>
> Romans 12:1-2 NASB

A transformed mind understands and approves the will of God. It perceives and thinks with the Kingdom in view. The word transformed is *metamorphoō*,[2] which is metamorphosis. We all know what happens to a caterpillar when it goes into metamorphosis. It becomes a new creation, a butterfly. The prefix, *meta*, is the same root as *metanoia*. This gives the picture of moving from thinking like an earth-bound caterpillar to thinking like a free-to-fly butterfly.

The root word is also the same as one used for transfiguration in Matthew 17:2. The transforming of the mind is the same as the transfiguration of Jesus on the mountain as Heaven saturated the whole place. Jesus revealed on the outside who He was on the inside—full of Heaven, full of life, and full of glory. *And we have the mind of Christ...*

THE ETERNAL CITY

The activation of our imagination to see and think as Jesus allows us to review the story of Abraham through this lens. If we reapproach his life from Heaven's view, we can start by asking, "What did Abraham do? What was so special about wandering around in the desert for a hundred years?" Yes, he believed in God, and it was credited to him as righteousness (Romans 4:3), but was there more to it? What was the fruit of walking in that kind of faith on the planet with a heavenly mentality for all those years?

> By faith Abraham, when he was called, obeyed by going out to a place which he was to receive for an inheritance; and he went out, not knowing where he was going. By faith he lived as an alien in the land of promise, as in a foreign land, dwelling in tents with Isaac and Jacob, fellow heirs of the same promise; for he was looking for the city which has foundations, whose architect and builder is God.

> Hebrews 11:8-10 NASB

He wasn't just wondering around in the desert. He was looking for the city which is designed and built by his Father. In doing so, he was transferring the blueprints for all who would walk this journey of faith after him. Essentially, his journey poured the foundation for such a city to be built on the Earth. This is the Eternal City. He saw it, believed it, and opened it up to the Earth.

IMAGINATION ACTIVATES FAITH.
IT IS CHOOSING TO SEE IT ON THE INSIDE
BEFORE YOU SEE IT ON THE OUTSIDE.

Abraham trusted his "faith sensory perception" (FSP) above natural counsel. His connection to his Father was preeminent in his life. It led to discoveries no one else was looking for. As Christians, it is easy to write off the Eternal City as something metaphorical. What if Abraham found his mystically Eternal City? What if that's where he met Melchizedek? What if we can find it too? What if it's all around us, inviting us to come and see?

When God called Abraham, he got a glimpse of something in the age to come and determined to pull it into his generation. Did he succeed? Yes. His wandering planted the seeds of faith for the City of Heaven to be built and expand in the Earth. Every one of faith enters-into, builds, and expands the city.

Abraham's call opened the eyes of his imagination to search for the Eternal City. In searching for it, he began to build it. The search and the build combined for him to experience it. He saw it before it was a reality, he built what he saw, then he experienced what he saw. When we see Heaven, Heaven downloads into us. It becomes our operating system, creating a template in our imagination to search for and build what we have seen. In doing so, we experience it.

When God speaks to us, His world is created within us. Past, present, and future are all alive in Jesus, who eternally exists outside of time and space. We construct through imagination what His voice reveals to us— overriding the temporal system with the eternal. This internal construction transforms our bodies, minds, and spirits. His word is alive in us, burning like a fire, consuming all we are until we become that which He spoke. What we've become on the inside, we will begin to experience on the outside, forging us into architects of the Kingdom. He creates His world within us, so we can recreate His world around us, building the City of Heaven on the Earth.

The City is unseen yet eternal. Despite the devil's best efforts and all the forces in the spiritual realms, this City continues to grow in each generation. It is the Mountain that is filling the Earth. It is not just a city but a Kingdom. We are emissaries of the City and ambassadors of the Kingdom.

> So then you are no longer strangers and aliens, but you are fellow citizens with the saints, and are of God's household, having been built on the foundation of the apostles and prophets, Christ Jesus Himself being the corner stone, in whom the whole building, being fitted together, is growing into a holy temple in the Lord, in whom you also are being built together into a dwelling of God in the Spirit.

> Ephesians 2:19-22 NASB

Apostles and prophets are builders—modern day Abrahams. They are the foundation in whom Heaven shines through for others to add to the building on top of the foundation they laid. Not all of us function specifically as apostles and prophets, but all of us are apostolic and prophetic. In order to build, you must recognize yourself as such. The recognizing brings the equipping. Knowing who you are in the Lord establishes your true identity. Any thoughts we have from Heaven towards Earth are apostolic and prophetic.

Historically, the church has misunderstood and oppressed imagination. This negative mindset is usually accompanied by the same accusatory mentalities who classify the supernatural as heretical. The church is the only entity on the Earth who can unlock the true power of imagination. Sadly, she has stepped on her own foot when it comes the role imagination plays in the transformed mind. However, there is an acceleration happening. She is awakening to her true identity. Don't fear those who don't understand you. Function in the love of the Father and the ones who oppose you today could be your biggest supports and friends tomorrow.

WHEN OUR IMAGINATIONS ARE FIRING AT HEAVEN'S CAPACITY, IT AWAKENS THE IMAGINATION IN OTHERS.

Through telling you of my encounters in Heaven, it automatically fills your imagination with the wonder my speech constructs. Does your heart say "yes" the invitation to taste and see? A "yes" in us is attractive to God. Where there is a "yes" in the Earth; Heaven chooses to come and inhabit it. With our "yes," we become the gateway to "Heaven invading Earth." God chooses our "yes" to Him and responds with "amen"—so be it! And when his "yes" is present within us, it will draw people to Him through us. We become the heavenly ecosystems that nourish the Earth. If Jesus lives in us, then those around us will see Him when they see us.

ACTIVATION

Our eyes give us depth perception to see in the natural. Our faith—eyes of our imagination—gives us perception (FSP) to see in the supernatural. I pray that the eyes of your spirit will become active. We always see with our spirit, but we are not always aware of it. The framework the eyes of the spirit transmit to us can be lost in the clutter of the natural. Find a place to be still in God's presence. Quiet your natural senses. Focus on the face of Jesus. As you begin to see, let your interaction be with Him alone. Don't second guess what you are seeing. Allow Holy Spirit to guide you into the encounter.

After you do this a few times, you will begin to navigate what Jesus is showing you and how to flow with the leading of the Holy Spirit. Seeing with our spiritual eyes will enhance what we see with our natural eyes. Remember, Heaven is the setting for Earth. If our faith sensory perception is active, then we will see the Earth through the lens of Heaven. Sight is singular where we see the reality of Heaven on Earth, and what is happening in the spirit, in the natural. Record your experience in a journal that expands as an ever-living encounter from this day forward.

DECLARATION

I will use my transformed mind to imagine the impossible. I am seated next to Jesus in the highest place in Heaven. There is nothing He cannot do. There is nothing that He cannot do through me. I am part of the Heavenly Family. I will rise as a revivalist in my generation. I will live my life as a demonstration of His Kingdom.

I will rise! I will revive! I will thrive. I am a revivalist!

RISE REVIVALIST!

NOTES

[1] *Zondervan NASB Exhaustive Concordance* (Zondervan, Grand Rapids, 1998). p. 1559.
[2] *Zondervan NASB Exhaustive Concordance*. p. 1547-1548.

CHARGE

Christianity is supernatural. It is the living body of Jesus. Everything about Jesus is perfectly supernatural. He is otherworldly. His people are otherworldly, which means that you and I are otherworldly. We are the ones who revive His original intention and design of the cosmos for all creation. We are the ones who see beyond the natural realm. We are sons and daughters of a good Papa who uses us to restore His prodigals to the Family and heal those who are hurting. We bring the supernatural answer everywhere we go, in everything we do, and to everyone we meet.

If I have been successful, this book has become a charge for you to rise as a revivalist, to take up the call, and transform your generation. Carry the Revivalist's anthem in your heart, and light the way for future generations.

RISE REVIVALIST!

ABOUT THE AUTHOR

David Edwards is a revivalist who ignites passion for the presence of God and heavenly encounters. He shares at gatherings, churches, and conferences with his bride, Allessia. Their heart is to transform culture through Kingdom Family.

David is a graduate of FIRE School of Ministry, and Allessia is a graduate of Bethel Atlanta School of Supernatural Ministry. They also serve on the team at GMA and their spiritual papa, Leif Hetland. They live near Atlanta, GA with their doggy, Rylee, and have been in ministry over 20 years.

INVITE

To invite David and Allessia to speak at your gathering, church, conference, or event; please visit their website at Revivalism.net.

ALSO AVAILABLE

Activating a Prophetic Lifestyle   Radical Purity

Made in the USA
Columbia, SC
23 November 2018